Chiara Vazzoler
The Scuola Grande di San Giovanni Evangelista

Guide Marsilio

Photographs
Cameraphoto, Venice

Photographic references
Fondazione Giorgio Cini (p. 13)
Soprintendenza Speciale per il Polo Museale
Veneziano - under concession of the Ministero
per i Beni e le Attività Culturali (pp. 50-51)
Washington, National Gallery of Art (p. 59)

Translated by
David Graham

Cover
*Scuola di san Giovanni Evangelista,
detail of the marble* septum, 1478-81
photo by Cameraphoto, Venice

Layout
Tapiro, Venice

© 2005 by Marsilio Editori® s.p.a.
in Venezia
First edition: November 2005
ISBN 88-317-8898-1

www.marsilioeditori.it

Reproduction in part or in whole by any means,
including photocopying, also for internal educational use,
is prohibited without specific authorisation

Contents

9 **The Scuola Grande di San Giovanni Evangelista: seven centuries of history**
  Michela Dal Borgo

11 Emblems of the Scuola
12 The *Scuola dei Battuti*
13 The *Mariegola* and the old institutional organisation of the Scuola
14 A *Scuola Grande* in grand Venice
17 The recent restorations

18 **Exterior**
21 The marble *septum*

Ground floor
24 Atrium
26 Hall of Columns / Lobby
29 Furnishings and other historic objects
30 The staircase

First floor
34 Hall of St John, or Chapter Room
41 St John the Evangelist: tradition and iconography
42 *Stories of St John the Evangelist*
45 The Cycle of the *Apocalypse*
48 Stucco Rooms (Sacristy and Chancellery)
50 The Relic of the Cross and the *Miracles*
    The *Miracles of the Cross*
52 Oratory of the Cross
55 The reliquary and the processional pole
56 The Albergo
59 Titian in the Scuola di San Giovanni Evangelista
60 Archive, or Guarana Room

63 **Essential bibliography**

Exterior

1. marble *septum*
2. *campiello*

ground floor

3. *atrium*
4. hall of columns
5. shrine of the dead
6. lobby
7. secretary's office
8. porter's room
9. library-records room
10. green room
11. grey room
12. staircase

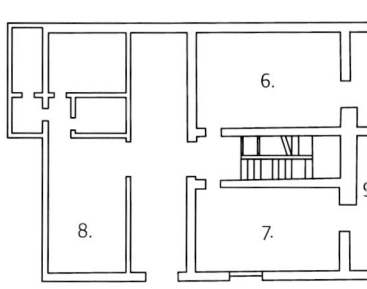

first floor

13. hall of st John, or chapter room
14. stucco room (chancellery)
15. stucco room (sacristy)
16. oratory of the cross
17. the albergo
18. archive, or Guarana room

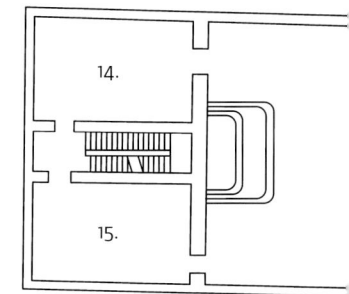

12.
5.
12.
11.
4.
3.
10.
1.
2.

18.
17.
16.
13.

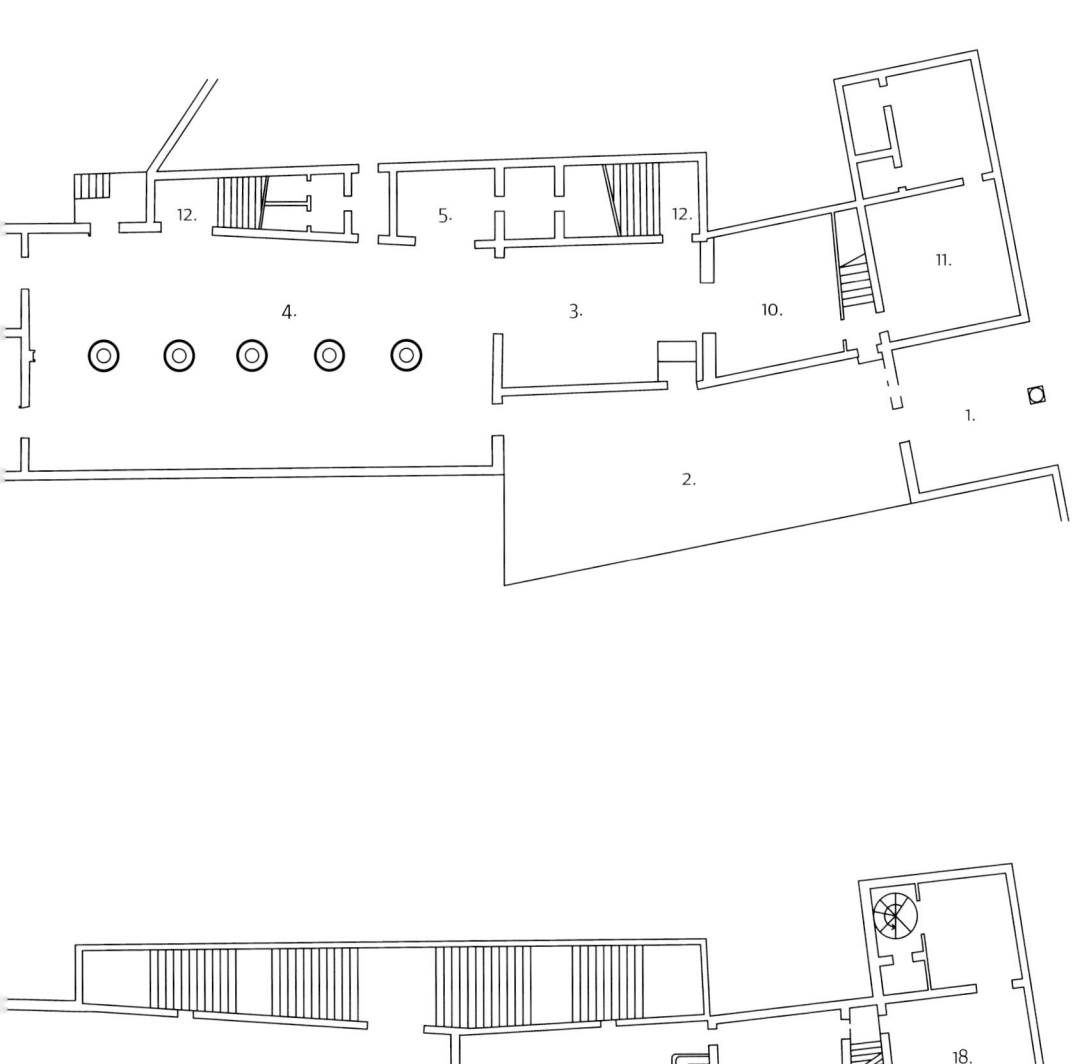

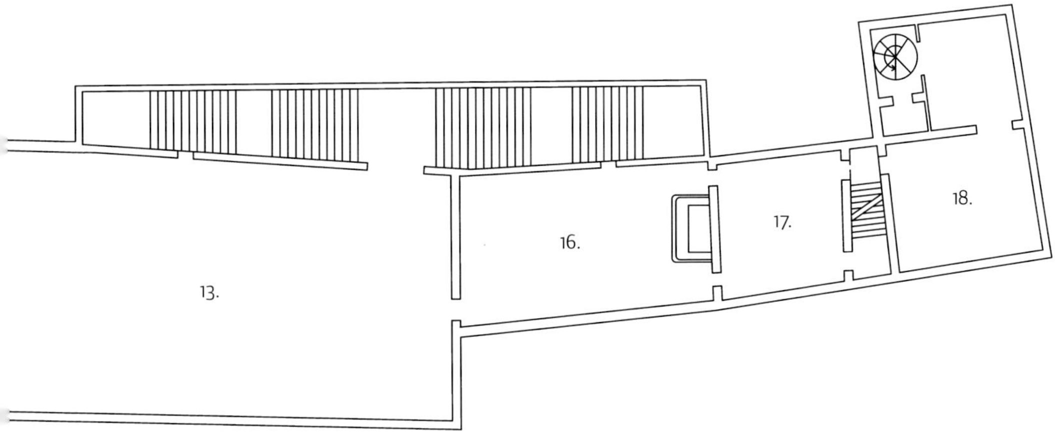

The Scuola Grande di San Giovanni Evangelista: seven centuries of history
Michela Dal Borgo

A *Fraternita di frari battuti*, *Fraternitade de disiplina*, or Brotherhood of Flagellants was formed in 1261 at the church of Sant'Apollinare (popularly Sant'Aponal), following the teachings of the hermit Raniero Fasani. It was the second of the brotherhoods after that of Santa Maria della Carità (1260, not reformed and now housing the Gallerie dell'Accademia), that from 1467 were known as *scolae magnae*, or *Scuole Grandi*. In 1301 it moved to the church of San Giovanni Evangelista – from which it took its name – in the parish of Santo Stefano confessore (popularly San Stin), and in October 1340 rented rooms on the first floor of the 'hospice' annex for poor and needy elderly women from the noble Badoer family, patrons of the church. As the number of brothers, its financial resources and religious prestige grew – with the acquisition of a precious fragment of the Holy Cross, donated in 1369 by the French knight Philippe de Mezières, grand chancellor of the Order of Jerusalem and Cyprus – the Scuola decided in around 1414 to build its own permanent premises. The result was a huge monumental complex on the currently occupied site, entrusted over three centuries to the invention of famous Lombard architects. The interior was gradually adorned with fine pictorial works commissioned by the brothers, among which the cycle of paintings on the miracles attributed to the relic of the Holy Cross by **Gentile Bellini**, **Vittore Carpaccio** and other masters stands out in particular.

The brotherhood's membership included citizens, merchants and artisans, and from its inception was placed under state control through the Council of Ten. It performed important devotional functions of assistance and charity over the centuries, and also gave tangible financial support, almost of a banking nature, to the treasury during emergency situations ('public loans'). The activities of the Scuola were all directed by a close circle of members, the *Banca*, elected by the General Chapter of brothers, which took in various institutional offices that are still partly covered by the existing *Capitolo di Banca e Zonta*.

When the Most Serene Republic of Venice fell on 12 May 1797, the Scuola retained its status until the revolutionary Napoleonic decree of 25 April 1806, which transferred its assets to public ownership, and that of 26 May 1807, which prohibited any kind of brotherhood or lay association. In 1814 the Austrian government turned the premises of the Scuola into a public warehouse for works of art taken from the various religious buildings that had been closed down. In order to save at least the architectural complex, the paintings and ancient archive having now been transferred, a special *Pia società per l'acquisto della Scuola Grande di San Giovanni Evangelista* (Holy Society for the acquisition of the Scuola Grande di San Giovanni Evangelista) was set up in 1855 on the initiative of Gaspare Biondetti Crovato. It consisted of 83 commendable private businessmen who the following year purchased it from the crown property of the Lom-

Domenico Tintoretto
St John survives the cup of poison (detail) 1623-26

bard-Veneto Kingdom for 30,000 Austrian lire, thus preventing its demolition – the area having already been designated for the construction of private housing by shrewd speculators.

A *Corporazione delle Arti Edificatorie di Mutuo Soccorso* (Mutual Aid Corporation of Building Arts) was then founded by the same purchasing members in 1856, based in the Scuola, whose statute included the old ideals of charity, devotional duties and mutual aid between the brothers. In accordance with its aims, the Pia Società ceded the property and the management of the building to the Corporazione delle Arti in 1877, which in 1892 took on the new name of *Società delle Arti Edificatorie di Mutuo Soccorso nella Scuola Grande di San Giovanni Evangelista* (Mutual Aid Society of Building Arts in the Scuola Grande di San Giovanni Evangelista).

In February 1929, at a special meeting, the Società decided to refound the ancient glorious association, resuming its name of Scuola Grande di San Giovanni Evangelista and asking the patriarch of Venice for canonical recognition. Pope Pius XI acknowledged the refounded Scuola Grande in the apostolic brief *Venetiarum in civitate* of 7 March 1931, conferring on it the honorary title of arch confraternity.

The early artistic patrimony produced by the Scuola Grande di San Giovanni Evangelista, now held in the Venice State Archives, consists of about 510 pieces, including busts, registers and parchments, with records of proceedings from 1261 to 1806; the nineteenth-century archives are still held at the Scuola itself.

In 2003 the Scuola Grande di San Giovanni Evangelista was awarded the international prize for the restoration of Venice, established by the Ateneo Veneto and dedicated to the person and memory of the engineer Pietro Torta, for: 'long-term actions aimed at conserving the ancient premises, restoring the centuries-old splendour of a monumental complex'.

Pietro Lombardo
Marble septum (detail)
1478-81

Emblems of the Scuola

The monogram 'SZ'. This stands for 'San Zane', which is Venetian dialect for St John the Evangelist, patron of the Scuola.

The crosier. The staff bent at its upper end, the symbol of the authority of the bishops, refers to the works of St John the Evangelist as head of the Christian community in Ephesus, in Asia Minor. The curve often takes on an allusive form of the Cross.

The eagle. Traditional symbol of St John the Evangelist, it derives from visions of the Revelation (chapter 4) and Ezekiel (chapter 1), like the symbols of the other apostles (the lion of Mark, the ox of Luke and the angel of Mathew) and refers both to the Ascension of Christ and to the heights reached by Johannine theology.

The chalice with snake. Traditional attribute of St John the Evangelist, it refers to the attempt to poison him in Ephesus. The poison touched by the saint miraculously fled in the form of a snake.

The book or books. Attribute of St John the Evangelist, as the writer of the Fourth Gospel and the Revelation, identified respectively as open and closed book.

The Cross. Universal symbol of Christianity, in the Scuola it refers specifically to the miraculous Relic of the Cross held by the brotherhood since 1369. The crosses depicted in the Scuola often refer more or less obviously to the form of the reliquary.

The *Scuola dei Battuti* (relief, 1349)
Built into the external wall facing the *campiello*, this relief is a significant presentation of the Scuola as a medieval brotherhood before its decisive acquisition of the Relic of the Cross. In 1349, immediately after the tragedy of the great black plague, the kneeling brothers turn to the patron saint who, standing upright, teaches and supports them (the guardian grande leans on his staff). The brothers are wearing their ceremonial cowl and are arranged into two rows led by candle bearers. They are depicted not so much in prayer, as in the acting out of a procession on their knees: the scourges they used to complete this penitence hang from their forearms. Founded in 1261, the Scuola was inspired by the movement of flagellants, founded in Perugia in 1260, which had promoted public self-flagellation as an act of penitence not only for personal redemption but also that of society as a whole. The distressing precariousness of man's material and spiritual destiny, particularly evident in the new urban, mercantile and artisan towns, was met 'with thankful mind and joyful spirit', as written in the *Mariegola*, a discipline for the salvation of souls founded on reciprocal prayer and charity. The inscription below (a twentieth-century copy, the original is in the foyer) announces *l'inizio del lavorier* ('start of works' in Venetian dialect): the refurbishing of the rooms let by the Badoers as the first premises of the Scuola. The event and the names of the participants are engraved on the stone as if it were a paper document, a scroll opened by two figures of kneeling brothers; the Gothic letters are in relief, according to a precious custom soon abandoned because of its delicacy and difficulty of execution. In the lunette above, a *Virgin and Child* indicate a devotion to Mary, an essential part of Venetian worship at the time also evident in other works commissioned by the Scuola in this period (a panel, now in the Sala dell'Albergo; the *Madonna of Humility*, now in the Gallerie dell'Accademia, and possibly also the lost cycle by Jacopo Bellini, at times described as the *Stories of the Virgin*).

The *Mariegola* and the old institutional organisation of the Scuola

In October 2003 the Scuola published a superb edition of its *Mariegola*: the collection of statutory rules that bring the sentiments that still inspire members of the Scuola even more to life. Brother Gian Andrea Simeone made the transcription of the parchment original held in the State Archives of Venice, starting from the year of foundation through to the end of 1457. He was also able to recompose sections that have been lost over the centuries. In particular he found two completely illuminated sheets, one now in the Cleveland Art Museum in Ohio, USA, and the other in the Marmottan - Claude Monet Museum in Paris, France. He also discovered the first page of the text, which is also decorated with illuminations and is held by the Giorgio Cini Foundation in Venice.

The ancient *Mariegola* (of which several copies exist) contains the founding statutes and rules of association registered over the centuries. In particular it dictated the conditions for admission to the Scuola. Candidates had to be male Venetian citizens by birth and at least 20 years old. It set the maximum number of brothers at 550 and laid down their duties. These included participation in the city's religious ceremonies in cowl and an obligation to help brothers in difficulty. In addition to attendance at funerals, prayers of intercession for the dead and assistance to the ill and dying, the works of charity were organised in various ways, such as the daily distribution of alms, annual dinners, provision of lodgings *amore Dei* (at symbolic rentals), the 'kindnesses' or contributions for the dowries drawn periodically for young women aspiring to marriage or being inducted into monastic orders. It also established a precise ceremony for the periodic elections of the governing members by the Chapter, the general assembly of brothers with voting rights, who were distinguished into *Banca* (the word derives from the banco (bench) near the altar in the various churches held by every brotherhood) and *Zonta*. The latter denominated those members added to the *Banca*, required by the Council of Ten, so that expansion of the few places available encouraged the election of candidates favoured by the Council. Considering the limited number of Scuole Grandi and their enormous political, economic and social weight, it may easily be understood that these oligarchies wielded considerable power, greater than that of the last of the many nobles who sat in the Great Council, and established alliances rather with the leading nobles.

The list of brothers (initially recorded in the *Mariegole*, then updated into special *libri mare*) were then divided into groups according to function and order of importance: *bancali*, the members of the *Banca*, including the *guardian grande* (chairman), the vicar, the chancellor, the *proto* (architect), the treasurer, the lawyer and the *guardian da mattin*; church ministers (chaplain, sacristan, music master) in varying numbers, normally paid, chosen from the convent clergy and the nearby parishes; nuns; although the question of the participation of women in the Scuole may be controversial, the spiritual contribution of the nuns, probably chosen according to customary and family ties, was certainly regarded as fundamental; servants led by a captain (the custodian), provided with a distinctive cowl and ceremonial staff, on public occasions; brothers in the service of the sick (doctors, barbers, visitors), for carrying out a qualified system of home medical visits, with prescriptions to be presented so that the costs of medicines could be charged to the brotherhood; nobles, although excluded from the administration of the Scuole Grandi, nevertheless had a prestigious role, often as patrons; brothers of the discipline: all the other brothers.

Mariegola of the Scuola Grande di San Giovanni Evangelista
XIV century, first page
Venice, Fondazione Giorgio Cini

A *Scuola Grande* in grand Venice

At the beginning of the modern age the brotherhood had taken on the typical profile of the *Scuole Grandi*, the most prominent urban institutions until the fall of the Republic. In the Veneto area all kinds of association were known by the name of *Scuola*, taking up the Greek term meaning a group of people who practise a discipline or follow a teacher. The brotherhoods dedicated to the patron saint of every corporation or professional art were Scuole, as were those named after the patrons of the various native countries of the resident foreigners in the city (e.g. Greeks, Dalmatians, Albanians), as were the synagogues. Other Scuole were dedicated to helping the needy (the blind, the lame, prisoners, the condemned, the 'humiliated' poor, or those poverty-stricken through unexpected circumstances) or were promoted by religious orders to encourage certain religious practices. From the middle ages to the fall of the Republic, more than 900 Scuole involved almost all Venetians in an organised network administered entirely by lay citizens. They were overseen by special state magistrates, who approved their constitutions, their statutes (*Mariegole*) and their balance-sheets, established the maximum number of members and provided for reforms and closures (especially in the eighteenth century) in the case of abuses. The scuole presented themselves as instruments of moral instruction and social control, because their material and spiritual benefits were conditional on respect for certain rules of behaviour (such as sobriety, not taking part in fights or armed violence). Other state laws, such as the prohibition against night meetings, were aimed at preventing the public and political disturbances that could result from the attendance of people from all classes, albeit with differing roles, in community activities. The highest state security body, the Council of Ten, set up to prevent sects and plots, dealt with the so-called Scuole Grandi, from 1622 through the *Inquisitori e Revisori sopra le Scuole Grandi*. This title originally covered only four Scuole (Santa Maria della Carità and San Marco founded in 1260, San Giovanni Evangelista in 1261 and Santa Maria della Misericordia or della Valverde in 1308, with links back to 1261), because they boasted the prestigious origins of the *Scuole dei Battuti*; that is, they were related to the flagellant movement of 1260, which was the highest authority for all the brotherhoods of northern Italy. The name was then given to other Scuole of different or later foundation (San Rocco in 1478, San Teodoro in 1552, Santa Maria del Rosario in 1675, Santa Maria della Consolazione e San Girolamo deputata alla Giustizia in 1689, Santa Maria del Carmine in 1767), which earned similar prestige for their wealth, membership and economic, religious and social importance, and had similar organisational aspects, including the rule that membership not be connected to any professional or national body. The Scuole Grandi took part in the city's social welfare system, developed over the centuries by a variety of private organisations and inspired by the principles of Christian charity (confraternities, hospitals and hospices, convents and holy places, in addition to the Scuole), and managed considerable financial and property assets, created by legacies and bequests, and made loans to the state, to whose finances they contributed to for emergency situations such as wars or famines. The ability of the *Scuole Grandi* to direct and organise the public economic and social forces of all classes made them the favoured partner of the republic as an essential tool for maintaining social equilibrium and control and obtaining political consensus. The ostentatious wealth of the Scuole in public processions was also a show of prosperity and support for the state, while their splendid premises vaunted works of art that, still *in loco* or in the museums of the world, remain some of the finest examples of the great periods of Venetian art. The Scuola di San Giovanni Evangelista is the only one of the first four Scuole Grandi to survive and this extraordinary longevity is evident in the building that has housed it since the beginning of the fourteenth century.

Antique strongbox

Construction

The first premises were created between 1349 and 1350 by rebuilding the dilapidated rooms on two floors of the old Ospizio Badoer, which Geremia Badoer di Filippo had granted to the Scuola in 1340. Although limited by the associational life of a Scuola that was not yet 'Grande', the works in any case defined both the site where the institution was to remain through to the present, opening onto the *campiello* at the front and bordering the canal at the back, and the important division between a colonnaded ground floor and an upper hall. The relief and inaugural epigraph from 1349 also remain from that period, as do possibly the capitals in the Hall of Columns on the ground floor.

Only 20 years later, in 1369, the acquisition of the prestigious Relic of the Cross boosted the devotional and economic importance of the Scuola. In 1389 it obtained full possession of the old hospice and committed itself to rebuilding it as soon as possible. An overall reconstruction project was thus launched (now testified by the Hall of Columns on the ground floor) with the addition of a second room on the first floor, the Oratorio della Croce, to house the relic in its superb Gothic reliquary. By the early years of the 1380s the decorations had been enhanced by important works such as the *Madonna of Humility* by **Giovanni da Bologna** (now in the Gallerie dell'Accademia). After 1420 the rooms were entrusted to the leading Venetian artist of the day, **Jacopo Bellini**, admitted as a brother in 1437, who painted the first of the famous Venetian cycles for the Scuola, no longer extant. This building programme ended in 1454 with the late Gothic arrangement of the *campiello* elevation, distinguished by the ogee windows of the Oratorio della Croce.

Capital with relief of brother, c. 1350

This second addition also has its epigraph, positioned below the previous one and dated 8 March 1453 (Veneto year, so actually 1454).

In the second half of the fifteenth century, with its prosperity and institutional standing now established, the Scuola Grande turned its attention to its outdoor spaces, with the arrangement of the church portico (freely represented in the canvas by **Lazzaro Bastiani** in the *Miracles of the Cross* cycle), and especially with the commission to **Pietro Lombardo's** stonemasons for the marble *septum* that distinguishes the whole San Giovanni Evangelista complex, crafted between 1478 and 1481. The entrance portal to the Hall of Columns, whose design is attributed to **Gentile Bellini**, could also date from this period (if not from the first years of the following century). All the main figures of the Venetian proto-Renaissance took their turn on the Scuola building site: in 1498 **Mauro Codussi** added the completely new volume of the staircase alongside the fifteenth-century building and also worked on the Chapter Room. Early in the following century, the biforate window facing the courtyard (above the entrance to the Hall of Columns) and a band of circular windows were opened here, as documented by Lazzaro Bastiani's canvas. At the same time the decorations were enhanced with the astonishing cycle of paintings with the *Miracles of the Cross* (1494-1502) by **Pietro Perugino**, **Vittore Carpaccio**, **Gentile Bellini** and others.

In the mid-sixteenth century, work focused on the Sala dell'Albergo, next to the Oratorio, reordered in the 1540s and furnished with its wooden panelling. Another very prestigious studio was commissioned for the ceiling, no longer *in situ*: that of **Titian**. In the 1580s **Jacopo Palma il Giovane** completed the pictorial decorations for the Albergo. In 1580 it had been decided that the now antiquated and shabby cycle by Jacopo Bellini be destroyed. Then, between the end of the century and the beginning of the following one, the cycle on the *Life of St John the Evangelist* (not entirely preserved) by **Domenico Tintoretto** and other representatives of the Veneto school was composed for the Chapter Room. The relentless pictorial production included minor episodes, such as the portraits of brothers by Tintoretto, now lost, in the lunettes on the monumental staircase.

Pietro Lombardo
Marble sept (detail)
1478-81

In 1727 the last big building programme began in the Scuola thanks to a bequest of 1697, directed by **Giorgio Massari** until the end of the 1770s, then continued by the students until the closure of the brotherhood in 1806. The work, including the restoration of the facade-arch by **Pietro Lombardo** (1731), started with the raising and lengthening of the Chapter Room, followed by extensions to the west (Sacristy and Chancellery) and the east (Archive Room). As a whole, the first floor interiors summarise the great cultural period of the Venetian eighteenth century: a masterly synthesis of architectural styles and of wooden and marble plastic scenes, bright rococo stuccoes and big canvases from the Venetian school (from **Giandomenico Tiepolo** to **Domenico Maggiotto**, by way of **Gaspare Diziani**, **Jacopo Marieschi** and **Jacopo Guarana**). Lavished even in its less visible recesses, such as the landings on the secondary staircase, the refined decorative style of the century was also applied on the ground floor of the west wing, where a fine section of terrazzo paving with the symbols of the Scuola remains.

The recent restorations
After the fall of the Republic and the Napoleonic decrees of 1806-7, the Scuola Grande was closed, the property taken into state ownership and numerous works of art sent to public museums or sold privately. The building was used to store confiscated works of art, so suffered less damage than others, but its historical and architectural features were completely neglected for decades. The urban revival stimulated by construction of the rail bridge (1846) prompted the Friulan building contractor, Gaspare Biondetti Crovato, to found the *Pia società per l'acquisto della Scuola Grande di San Giovanni Evangelista* in 1855. This then raised the 30,000 Austrian lire needed to buy the building in order to make it the definitive home of the *Corporazione delle Arti Edificatorie di Mutuo Soccorso*. Biondetti's initiative made the monumental complex an active part of the urban renewals of subsequent decades, in particular the new pedestrian thoroughfares to and from the railway station (1858), the council's Recovery and Regulatory Plan of 1891 and the new urbanisation of the San Rocco area carried out by the Istituto Autonomo delle Case Popolari at the end of the century. In the meantime, upgrading of the building's artistic aspects proceeded through the instruction of boys in art and crafts in the Scuola by the Pia società and rental of the rooms to sculptors and painters. It was also the topic of discussions and fundamental works of historiography and art criticism: *Le fabbriche e monumenti cospicui di Venezia* (1838) offers the first survey of the marble screen designed by Leopoldo Cicognara, while *L'architettura e la scultura del rinascimento a Venezia* (1893) by the historian Pietro Paoletti bases the discovery of the genius of Mauro Codussi on archive materials.
The restorations continued slowly but assiduously throughout the twentieth century, interrupted only by the two Wars, thanks to personal donations and members' legacies. In 1948 a liberal plastic arts school was set up on the ground floor, whose teachers included Carlo Scarpa, Mario Deluigi and Umbro Apollonio.
In 1966 Alessandro Marcello was guardian grande. He belonged to the same family that had inherited the Reliquary of the Cross (previously taken into state ownership then rescued by the preceding guardian grande) and in 1929 had returned it to the Scuola through the patriarch of Venice, to seal the process of reconstructing its associative identity.
The big 'high water' of November in that year led to a marked improvement in the works, coordinated by the proto, Virgilio Vallot (1901-82), who in 1923 had been one of the first students of the new Istituto Superiore di Architettura di Venezia and taught at the Università d'Ingegneria in Padua. He was assisted by Giorgia and Angelo Scattolin, also among the first students and then teachers at the school. The Scuola, where the high water had reached the considerably high level marked with a notch on the first column in the ground floor Sala, became in these dramatic circumstances a workshop for a new conception of restoration and protection for the city's monuments. A study and documentation office was set up in the Sacristy and Chancellery for the committees to 'save' Venice, in association with the Soprintendenza ai Monumenti, Italia Nostra, Unesco and the Venice Committee (subsequently Save Venice). Between 1969 and 1971 a solution for protecting against high waters that is now in general use was applied for the first time on the ground floor. The architect Vallot built a complete drainage system to cope with high water, rising by filtration from the spongy subsoil or entering as the overflow from outside, based partly on ancient Paduan traditions of hydraulic engineering. The original supports for the five Gothic columns were exposed with the construction of circular stone tanks at the base of each column.
The subsequent works of repair and modification were directed towards the public functions the Scuola was taking on as a strategic choice for its conservation and appreciation. For decades the Scuola has been a prestigious venue between the city centre and the mainland for concerts, conferences, courses and cultural events. In the 1980s the IUAV History of Architecture Department was established in the Palazzo PBadoer and its Phototopographical Survey Laboratory made the first scientific survey of Codussi's staircase. The proto, Francalancia, directed the upgrading of the internal and external masonry structures while his successor, the architect Marino Vallot, along with the guardian grande, Gianni Capovilla, completed the repair of all the rooms. The Archive Room and some rooms decorated with stuccoes have been restored in recent years with the cooperation of the professional training courses for restorers held by the Istituto Veneto per i Beni Culturali, housed in the Scuola since 1996. The art of restoration, intended not only as the rightful conservation of the monument but also as an opportunity for promotion and progress, is a distinctive mark of the Scuola and its most substantial contribution to Venice, thanks also to numerous partnerships, many of them international.

Exterior

The Scuola di San Giovanni Evangelista is marked by its lack of a facade. For seven centuries the building has actually grown by way of continued extensions on the site of the original fourteenth-century edifice, while the surrounding urban area has become gradually busier, gravitating around the Franciscan Frari complex up until the nineteenth century, and then assailed by flows of pedestrians going to and from the mainland. The presence of the Scuola in the narrow, medieval *calli* is marked by the astonishing marble *septum* by **Pietro Lombardo** (1481), a proto-Renaissance masterpiece that highlights all of the building behind, visible through the central portal and two windows. In 1553 a pillar decorated with the symbols of the Scuola was also placed in the *campiello* in front of the *septum* to display the field standard, as was normal at all of the Scuole. The *campiello* has elegant paving dating from 1759, with geometric inlays of Istrian stone, but with the same dimensions and layout as the medieval courtyard it is based on. Indeed, it is overlooked by various buildings of diverse date and style that make up the Badoer complex. The generosity and sponsorship of this ancient noble family were fundamental to the development of the Scuola.

The left wall, bell tower and, further back, the Gothic apse of the *church* dedicated to St John the Evangelist are on the left of the *campiello*. Founded in 970 and rebuilt in the fifteenth century, then altered several times, the church has been marked by its various functions: as the patrician chapel of the Badoer family and as place of worship for the brotherhood, which provided it with its pictorial and plastic decorations carried out in the seventeenth and eighteenth centuries by the same artists who worked in the Scuola. At the end on the side, towards the portico that marks off the *campiello*, a door decorated with the crosier of St John, the symbol of the Scuola, leads to a colonnaded vestibule. The space in front of the church, originally open and traditionally used as a *cemetery* (the subject of controversy between the family and the Scuola), was subsequently incorporated into the Badoer family *palazzo* above. The elegant tracery of the seventeenth-century windows on two levels above the portico only partly reveals the main body of the building, with the traditional noble hall on the first floor. The *palazzo* is also lacking any real identifying facade, an anomaly not compensated for by its considerable bulk, which is arranged in a Z-shape along the *calle* and around another courtyard in the area behind, in the direction of the Frari. The Calle della Lacca, leading out of the *campiello* through the Sottoportico Vitalba, is straddled a little further on by the Ospizio Badoer, a small, typical, Venetian welfare organisation (still operating as a home for the elderly) founded on the basis of a legacy to provide accommodation for some needy elderly women and rebuilt here in the fifteenth century after the Scuola had taken over its original rooms on the *campiello*.

The other two elevations that define the *campiello* on the right side and the back (next to the Palazzo Badoer) belong to the Scuola, where elements that identify the main building works carried out can be read. On the side, of mainly medieval appearance: the relief with the brothers and the epigraph below, relating to the fourteenth-century building, and the late-Gothic windows of the fif-

Gabriel Bianco Zanne and **Andrea Buora** (design **Gentile Bellini**, attr.)
Entrance portal, c. 1512

teenth-century reconstruction; on the small end facade: the eighteenth-century oval window and the proto-Renaissance combination of Codussi's biforate window (pre 1512) above the entrance door to the Hall of Columns. This is a mock-classical caprice on two registers (the arch supported by two columns is surrounded by two small columns that support a lowered pediment) that is hypothetically attributed to **Gentile Bellini**, but also to the proto **Gabriel Bianco** and to **Zanne** and **Andrea Buora**.

The marble *septum* (1478-81)
The extraordinarily scenic art of **Pietro Lombardo** (1435-1515) produced an unexpected architectural invention in this isolated part of the city, whose typically Renaissance surface is a magnificent synthesis of structures and surfaces. Lightened by the three openings at the back, the screen extends into two lateral wings, also tripartite, creating an ideal, perfectly square space that is a fine example of geometric precision and proto-Renaissance classicism. The vertical lines of the fluted pilaster strips and the horizontal ones of the plinth and cornice rationally divide up the very restrained composition of marble surfaces. The Corinthian capitals, the frieze that runs along the entablature, the torches on top, the marble inlays and floral cornices then all enrich this harmonious backdrop. The two windows with pediments, enriched with Corinthian elements and floral cornices, flank the portal with its curved crown above. Some identifying symbols of the Scuola are concentrated here: the eagle and books, the attributes of St John, in the lunette; the Cross inserted in the terrestrial globe at the top, in reference to the relic housed in the Scuola. At the sides, kneeling on the entablature, two angels worship the instrument of redemption borne witness by the Evangelist. The pictorial presentation is completed with the words of the epigraph beneath: 'Divo Ioanni Apostolo et Evangelistae protectori et sanctissimae cruci', while the eagle reappears on the jambs.

Atrium

A large atrium is reached from the *campiello* by way of the side door on which a *Bust of St John the Evangelist* keeps watch. It dates from the fifteenth-century building, of which there is a reminder in the ceiling with exposed beams and spiral perimeter decoration. This passage area gives access to the various functional parts of the Scuola: the Renaissance staircase rises directly to the upper floor from right in front of the entrance, introduced by the imposing doorway on two fluted, Corinthian pillars and fine architrave niellated like a jewel (the incisions are filled with a black metal alloy of silver, copper, lead and sulphur); the mock classical doorway on the right leads to some service rooms in the east wing (the Green Room and Grey Room, which can also be reached by another small doorway on the *campiello* giving onto another staircase that leads to the 'offices' of the Albergo and the Archivio on the upper floor); on the left, the atrium joins the Hall of Columns (connected to the west wing) through an opening grandly squared by composite pillars on high plinths surmounted by a wooden architrave with the eagle of St John.

There are some reminders of the history of the building in this vestibule: the originals of the stone inscriptions relating to the first buildings are in front of the entrance (the ones in the *campiello* are early twentieth-century copies): the long scroll held by two brothers documents the start of works in 1349 and the square stone with crosiers the rebuilding of 1454. On the opposite wall there are five stones of the Corporazione delle Arti Edificatorie di Mutuo Soccorso, two of which carry bronze portraits: of Gaspare Biondetti Crovato, who was responsible for saving and reviving the building, and of the benefactor Augusto Agazzi.

The stone bas relief with the *Resurrection*, attributed to the **workshop of Antonio Rizzo** (fifteenth century), from a demolished Barbarigo monument, was not originally in the Scuola but is part of a small collection of stone materials of various provenance that also decorate the walls of the adjoining Hall of Columns, whose fittings date from the restorations following the big high water of 1966.

Mauro Codussi
Staircase entrance, 1498

Hall of Columns / Lobby

The Hall of Columns was intended for assemblies of the brothers and pilgrims. It retains the overall medieval aspect of the building updated in the early fifteenth century following the acquisition of the prestigious Relic of the Cross. It was restored after the big high water of 1966 and is distinguished by the row of five stone columns with lowered bases that support the long cross-beam bearing the exposed ceiling beams. Resembling a ship's keel, it charts the techniques and forms of Venetian civil architecture of the period (primarily of the Palazzo Ducale). So although the building is quite evidently invested with religion, from the outset it has had the typical civic character of the Scuole that were distinguished as 'Grandi' by the state institutions, not the ecclesiastical ones. The squared proportions are softened by the typical Venetian Gothic decorations, in particular by the cord-like border that runs along the edge of the ceiling and the centre beam, the corbels that discharge its weight onto the columns and the simple owl's beak Gothic capitals, possibly dating from the first building of 1350. Two relief images alternate on each side of every capital: the figure of a kneeling brother with cowl (according to the iconography already seen in the fourteenth-century relief outside) and the crosier of St John (a symbol that alludes to his work as bishop in Ephesus). These stone symbols on the columns that support the building recall the spiritual values underpinning the entire associative life: mutual prayer and the intercession of the saint, as described in the *Mariegola*, the association's statute.

Water entrance (detail)

Past the entrance towards the *campiello* (corresponding to the external Renaissance doorway), various openings lighten the severe medieval walls: the squared windows facing the *calle* (southern side) are from the Gothic period, as is the charming water entrance towards the back corner of the opposite wall, decorated outside with a cornerstone portraying two brothers at the sides of the Cross; while both the trabeated doorway (twin of the one in the atrium) and the small *Shrine of the Dead*, framed by two large pillars surmounted by a lowered arch with the crosier of St John, belong to the Renaissance stairway. The shrine retains an altar with a late fifteenth-century marble *tabernacle* from the church of Sant'Aponal, while the walls are lined with *stones* bearing the names of brothers and benefactors from 1856 to 1969. The *baluster* and *small gate* in bronze with the symbols of the four evangelists and the Cross date rather from the beginning of the twentieth century and are by **Carlo Lorenzetti**. The chapel and lateral spaces highlight the extraordinary composition of brick vaulting that supports the staircase; a door leads to the garden.

Most of the various *lapidary materials* on the walls are not originally from the Scuola but were acquired from various sources after the building had been stripped (many of them collected for educational purposes by the Società delle Arti Edificatorie di Mutuo Soccorso). The *Dead Christ* in the small Gothic shrine, with traces of colour on the small tortile columns, stands out among the group at the left of the entrance (three sculptures with figures of friars or monks, a pat-

Hall of Columns

era with animal decoration, two brackets with vegetable decoration, a tondo on square with a relief of a lamb, an inscription relative to 1393). The two tondi with St John's crosier are of historic interest. They are examples of the decorative elements normally used to distinguish the buildings owned by the brotherhood. Continuing along the south wall in an anti-clockwise direction, there are: a half figure with scroll, a trapezoidal bas relief from the fourteenth century portraying *St Martin, Doge Andrea Contarini and a monk* (with Gothic inscription recalling the 1378 war of Chioggia), the impressive *Madonna della Misericordia*, a Gothic high relief with traces of colour from the demolished church of Santa Lucia, a *St Peter*, a tondo attributed to the **Bon workshop** and a lunette with the *Holy Father, dove and angels*; on the end wall, *St Laurence Giustiniani* (first patriarch of Venice), an eighteenth-century sculpture with inscription, a fifteenth-century *St Anthony* in a Gothic niche with the monogram 'IHS', a Gothic cusp with a *Dead Christ* attributed to **Michele da Firenze**, a *Benedictory saint* and a stone with decorative elements and central hole. This group is ended by an interesting eighteenth-century *epigraph* of the *Corporazione dei burchieri and dei cavacanali* (canal maintenance workers). There is a Renaissance fireplace surround with vegetable decoration and coats of arms on the north wall.

The Hall of Columns provides access to a room connecting to the administrative offices where there is a fine eighteenth-century terrazzo floor featuring a big emblem of the Scuola (comprising a monogram with the letters 'SZ' and the crosier). This traditional flooring technique consists of scattering small fragments of coloured marble over a bed of several layers of powdered marble, earthenware and lime, ensuring the flexibility necessary for the constant settling of Venetian buildings. This unexpectedly elegant floor was uncovered during recent restorations to the west wing.

Urn for ballots

Furnishings and other historic objects

The Scuola has a significant collection of objects, furnishings and documents that speak of its history and traditions. These include an antique safe, various liturgical vestments and an original *urn for ballots* (used for drawing votive offerings or 'kindnesses').

The group of *procession equipment* dating mainly from the eighteenth and nineteenth centuries, made to previous models, is of particular importance and reflects the resolute observance of religious and civic ritual in which the Scuole Grandi played a central role for centuries. There were numerous public parades in Venice in which the brotherhoods, and through them the entire city, showed off their material wealth and declared their religious devotion: funeral processions and 'order' feasts (i.e. of the Scuola itself), civic and ecclesiastical holidays (ducal processions, the Redentore, Corpus Domini etc.) and occasional processions (such as to celebrate an escape from the plague or a war victory). The Scuole participated with a varying number of brothers and relics according to the importance of the brotherhood and the procession, and to state directives, using more or less complex procession equipment. Some typical elements were:

the *procession pole*, in wood, without stand, usually decorated with gilt inlays in the upper section. From 1371 the Scuola di San Giovanni was able to show off its precious Gothic reliquary held up on the big inlaid wooden pole, numbered among the oldest objects of its kind and also having the function of a pennant;

the *penelo* (or pennant), sign of the brotherhood, carved or in the form of a standard, with the image of the patron saint. The pennant and standard of the Scuola, recently restored and possibly dating from the end of the eighteenth century, depicted St John protecting the kneeling brothers on one side, and St John receiving the vision of the Revelation on the other;

the *solèr*, a kind of palanquin on which decorative elements representing Biblical scenes or other religious subjects were arranged. The Scuola has a magnificent eighteenth-century example, painted in red and gold, with the Johannine symbols of the eagle and books. It is set up for carrying the reliquary at the centre, with big candles at the corners;

the *baldachin*, a quadrangular decorated cloth for covering the *solèr* or other objects carried in procession, supported by four or more poles (as can be seen in the painting by Gentile Bellini). As well as the *solèr*, the Scuola has two sets of poles, one in decorated metal with engravings, the other in wood with mother-of-pearl inlays.

These materials, like the numerous big candles, were carried by *sfadiganti*, or drudges, poor brothers or hired help, equipped with special supports, like the *big leather belts with pocket in front*.

Only the most important Scuole were distinguished by the cowls worn by the brothers at ceremonies according to the ancient tradition of the flagellants. Some may still be admired at the parish festivals and during the Corpus Domini and St Mark's festivities in the basilica. The cowl of the Scuola di San Giovanni is white, with the symbols of the Cross and the crosier in red, and a cord to fasten the sides, with a vague suggestion of the ancient scourge.

Chalice, aspergilum and solèr

The staircase

Two wide trabeated openings give access from the entrance hall and the Hall of Columns to the superb double Renaissance staircase (1498), one of the masterpieces in the Scuola and an extraordinary example of the work of **Mauro Codussi** (1440-1504) of Bergamo.

In 1495, after having given the Gothic building its unusual Renaissance facade by the celebrated **Pietro Lombardo**, the brotherhood decided to build an access stairway of suitable quality to the *piano nobile*, appointing Codussi, who in the same years had taken over from Lombardo on the rival building site of the Scuola Grande di San Marco, where he had also built a double staircase (demolished in 1812 and subsequently rebuilt). But it was not at all easy to build an impressive staircase *de piera di fuoravia* (outside, in stone), when the land available (obtained from the Marin Zane family after drawn-out negotiations) was not much more than the dubious bank of the Rio di San Giovanni, which flows behind the Scuola, and furthermore in an area long known as a *lacus*, or swamp. The staircase actually brushes the water, as can be seen from the window in the approach to the Hall of Columns: a small corner of rare, purely Venetian harmony, where stone and water merge, creating constantly changing effects of light during the day and throughout the seasons. The *Moro murer* ('mason', as Codussi appears in the lists of brothers, registered by recognition according to the customs of the Scuola towards its own artists) displayed extraordinary skill in concealing a very difficult balance of forms and materials with its clear, sober lines: about 35 metres long, the staircase rises like a bridge to 12 metres, managing even to house in its span the chapel for the intercession of the dead, along with other large spaces.

Mauro Codussi
Staircase, 1498

Codussi circumvented the problem of limited space by exploiting the great discovery of the Renaissance: perspective. The system of lines converging toward a focal point, invented to represent the three-dimensional space of flat surfaces, was here used by the architect to add to the real space by optical illusion. This effect was obtained by widening the inside walls of the staircase towards the stairhead (the steps at the top are about 70 centimetres wider than at the base), so that the perspective lines of the stairs more noticeably diverge and converge (according to whether one stands at the top or the bottom), giving an illusion of greater depth. This altered perception is reinforced by elements that slow down the vista: the two spaces covered with blind domes at the beginning of the flights, the landings that interrupt the path, the side windows that punctuate the ascent and especially the small arches on hanging capitals that cross the barrel ceiling. Decorated with rosettes and the symbols of the Scuola, these delicate architectural elements are on the other hand needed to lend gradual adaptation to an only apparently

simple ceiling: it is actually resting on walls that diverge and stand on fairly swampy ground. The light also serves to create space. Captured in great quantities by the windows and lightly tinted by the water of the canal, the natural daylight glances over the barrel ceiling and expands onto the cladding of the white marble preferred by Codussi, which so clearly define the Renaissance architecture of the staircase compared to the wood and stone Gothic rooms on the ground floor. The soaring lines of the two flights of stairs culminate in the very elegant blind dome at the top resting on a drum delicately decorated with niello (a technique consisting of gluing a paste of metals into the engravings, creating an elegant design of black on white). Here, too, Codussi managed to overcome the constricted space (note the reduced dimensions of the drum of the dome), opening it up with four big arches, two facing the stairs, one the entrance to the Chapter Room and the other crowning the big window. The mock-classical decorative elements help to give depth and importance to the room: the wide lacunar soffits with rosettes, the double columns with Corinthian capitals and the small pillars with candlesticks; in short, the whole repertoire of the Renaissance competes here to qualify the landing as a refined anteroom for the big main hall.

Frieze of Building Arts (detail) 1856

The biforate window, an authentic 'trademark' of the master (indeed, it was Codussi who introduced the Tuscan model of the bifora with round arches and *oeil-de-boeuf*, known as *Codussiana*, to Venice and developed it, in place of the traditional curved, trefoil and multifoil windows), faces onto the small garden and gives the landing the airiness of a loggia: almost out of proportion (note the arch at a tangent to the drum of the dome), it is distinguished by its central column in refined dark grey marble which increases the effect of backlight and thus reduces the visual obstruction.

Not by chance, the members of the nineteenth-century Società per le Arti Edificatorie di Mutuo Soccorso wanted to add their own mark to the base of this 'signature' of the great Renaissance architect, and did so in the form of a *frieze* on the paving, with *putti* portraying the various building arts. In front, right on the threshold of the hall, another frieze carries the date the building was rescued, returned from Austrian state ownership in 1856, and other decorations with the professional tools of the association.

Hall of St John, or Chapter Room

The Renaissance staircase leads into the main hall of the building, known as the 'Capitolare' (Chapter Room) as it was used for the general assembly of the brothers eligible to vote. Like the Sala del Maggior Consiglio in the Ducal Palace and like the halls on the *piani nobili* of the patrician *palazzi*, the Chapter Room in all the Scuole Grandi is a reception area where the magnificence and importance – also political – of the brotherhood is shown off.

At the end of the seventeenth century, the old fifteenth-century hall with its low wooden lacunar ceiling decorated in gold and blue (similar to the ceiling in the current first room of the Gallerie dell'Accademia, formerly the Chapter Room of the Scuola Grande di Santa Maria della Carità) and the altar dedicated to the patron saint, also in wood, must have seemed inadequate to requirements. Round windows had been opened up during the Renaissance works, but in 1580 it had been decided to do away with the original paintings by Jacopo Bellini (registered as a brother, Bellini received a contribution for the dowry of his daughter Nicolosia who married Mantegna), which was the first series of Venetian paintings. They were in poor condition and no longer in keeping with contemporary taste. The whole ensemble was evidently unable to compete with the equivalent halls in the other Scuole, in particular with the majestic sixteenth-century cycles by Tintoretto in the nearby San Rocco, and did not satisfy one of the basic requirements for the title of Scuola Grande: the boast of monumental premises.

So the hall and then gradually the whole *piano nobile* was subject to a radical late Baroque reworking that continued throughout the following century. The main works were carried out between 1727 and 1762 under the direction of the architect **Giorgio Massari**, of proven skill in the difficult art of upgrading the oldest buildings in Venice. Massari created a highly effective, bright and elegant space by radically restoring the masonry structures and paying careful attention to the detail of all surfaces and furnishings.

The *coloured marble floor* (designed in 1732, but laid in 1752 to ensure it would not be damaged by the scaffolding needed to decorate the ceiling) is an absolute masterpiece. The red, black and white check pattern, typical of precious floors since the sixteenth-century (as seen in representations of the Last Supper, for example), is interwoven with oval and star-shaped geometric forms. Scanned by three big rosettes, the floor extends and unfolds in numerous inlays, each of which is a single piece allowing the geometric composition to conform to a space that, like many Venetian rooms of medieval origin, is not at all regular (as may be seen by observing the corners of the ceiling). A two-coloured band divides the complex pattern into three even sections, repeating on the floor the design of the lacunars on the ceiling, a pattern also found on the contemporary wooden benches along the walls.

Massari employed several stratagems to make the hall more impressive, being unable to expand it outwards. The ceiling, originally at the level of the horizontal entablature, was raised about five metres and the twelve big *oval windows* opened. These capture the light from above the surrounding roofs, making it fall in bands towards the floor and thus highlighting its colours and lustre. In order to

Giorgio Massari
*Hall of St John,
or Chapter Room*
1727-62

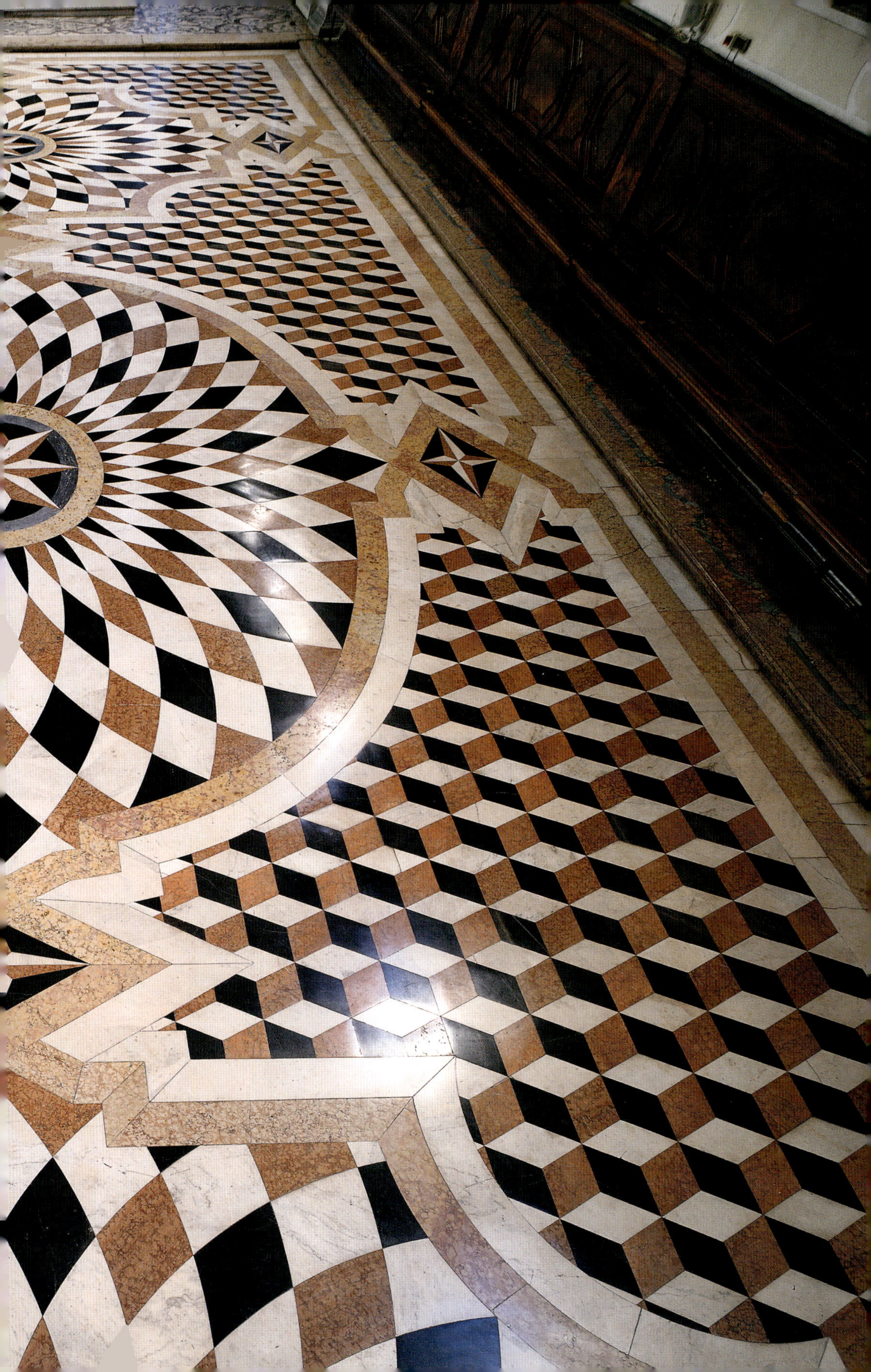

ALTARE PRI IN PERPETUO

avoid visual encumbrances, the *rococo decoration* is discreet, limited to the small pillars between the windows and the corresponding hanging capitals with acanthus leaves on the cornice below. The smooth walls are rationally ordered by the frames of the pictures and the long horizontal line of the wooden bench.

The impressive *altar* on the end wall is positioned on a tribune squared by two fluted, Corinthian half columns. The line of the architrave and a slight difference in floor level separate this part of the hall without disrupting its volume; rather extending it. The tribune is also distinguished by the colour of the floor, in refined tones of grey and violet, and the ribbon motif is also repeated. In this extremely elegant and well-proportioned space, even this enormous altar is lightened. In pale marbles with grey veining, it was designed by Massari in 1728 and built in 1729 by the stonemasons **Alvise** and **Francesco Rizzo**, **Bartolomeo Corbetto** and the engraver **Francesco Medici**. The altar itself was the reason for the works to upgrade the hall, thanks to a bequest by the brother Giacomo Pin in 1697, commemorated by an inscription at bottom left near the altar. Overcoming the difficulties presented by the previous Gothic building on swampy ground, Massari installed this marble work of considerable volume on the upper floor (the basement below has however been reinforced several times, also recently): four columns on high plinths support a double pediment surmounted by a lunette with central eye. In the middle, the niche framed by two small Doric columns houses the robust statue of *St John the Evangelist*, by **Giovanni Maria Morlaiter** (1732-33). The saint with pen and book in his hands is shown in the act of writing the gospel, flanked by the eagle and a cherub, the symbol of divine inspiration. The draped figure makes a rotary movement, turning his gaze upwards to where a skylight provides a band of light, giving the whole arrangement a certain theatrical quality.

In addition to the oval windows, some Codussi biforate windows were skilfully arranged to visually take up the original model of the staircase. There are two eighteenth-century windows at the sides of the tribune, while the bifora looking onto the courtyard was already in place on the opposite side of the hall, inserted by 1512. With a neo-classical sense of symmetry, Massari opened up another one that looks onto the oratory, removing one of the two small medieval doors and transforming the hall into a multi-functional open space, in which the visual field ranges unhindered from the altar of St John to that of the Cross in the oratory. The gaze can almost bound from one bifora to another, from one end of the hall to the other and also into the adjacent spaces of the oratory and the staircase.

The remaining door to the oratory is enhanced by appropriate decoration that takes up the pattern of the fluted half columns already used to mark the tribune and extends into the attic above, made up of pediment and cornice and crowned with the eagle flanked by two torches. The bas relief by **Giovanni Maria Morlaiter**, contemporary with the statue of the saint on the opposite side of the hall, marks the *Donation of the Relic of the Cross*. The eighteenth-century taste for Morlaiter's slightly bombastic plastic forms paradoxically expresses the spirit of the fourteenth-century events, in that the relic arrived

Alvise and **Francesco Rizzo**
Bartolomeo Corbetto
Francesco Medici
(design **Giorgio Massari**)
Altar of St John, 1729

Giovanni Maria Morlaiter
St John the Evangelist
1732-33

in 1369 amid great pomp and celebration, with a major ceremony involving both civil and religious authorities.

The large but balanced assembly hall measures 34.5 metres in length, 13 in width and 11 in height. In line with eighteenth-century sensibilities, it also has perfect natural acoustics, enhanced by the lacunar ceiling, which make it one of the best halls for chamber music in the city.

The pictorial decorations centre on the patron saint of the Scuola. Most of the paintings on the walls were commissioned at the end of the sixteenth century to replace the worn out cycle by Bellini and focus on *Episodes from the life of St John the Evangelist*, taken from the *Golden Legend* of Jacopo da Varagine, which gathers various traditions. They deal with the subject of St John's preaching in Ephesus and his victorious fight against paganism.

Bust of St John the Evangelist early XV century

The *ceiling* (1760-62) has a cycle of scenes from the book of Revelation, whose author, John, in exile on the island of Patmos, is traditionally identified with the same John who wrote the fourth Gospel. The canvases also reproduce various verses from the Bible, something quite rare in this subject, though without respecting their order, here dictated by aesthetic and functional requirements. The big wooden sections designed by Massari were intended for the 'grand manner' of Giambattista Tiepolo, who was to have been commissioned to paint at least the central canvas (if for no other reason than to respond to the sumptuous ceiling he had painted 20 years earlier for the Scuola Grande dei Carmini). At the time, the idea of engaging Massari as architect, Morlaiter as sculptor and Tiepolo as painter meant putting together a trio of the highest prestige, an ambition, though, that in some ways eluded the brotherhood. The now elderly painter preferred the court of Madrid to yet another Venetian commission and left the city in 1762. Despite the absence of Venice's most famous artist, the ceiling of the San Giovanni Evangelista is a very effective group. It is a kind of 'anthology' of Venetian decorativism of the second half of the eighteenth century, with sections by the most famous artists of the period, also active abroad, and two magnificent contributions by **Giandomenico Tiepolo** in the corner sections towards the oratory.

St John the Evangelist: tradition and iconography

As well as the numerous symbols, there are two main iconographies of the patron saint, both represented in the Scuola. The fourteenth-century works reflect the Byzantine influence on Venetian art and show St John as an old, balding man with beard and cloak, corresponding to the canons of wisdom and dignity appropriate to an apostle, and the tradition of his longevity. This is how the saint is shown in the *relief of the Battuti*, in the panels of the Albergo and at the Accademia, on the back of the reliquary, and again in the *bust* above the early fifteenth-century entrance. Western art then elaborated a second model that emphasises the disciple's virginity; he was considered the youngest of the apostles. On the spectacular altar in the Chapter Room, the rich drapery of his clothing, his languid pose and long hair in ringlets give the patron an appearance that is certainly not particularly virile, conforming not only to this tradition but also to eighteenth-century taste. St John in exile in Patmos also remains an old, bearded man in western iconography, as he was depicted by **Titian** and **Palma il Giovane** in the cycle for the Albergo. So the iconography of the young John in the eighteenth-century cycle of the *Apocalypse* is quite anomalous. He seems to retain the features of the figure in the sixteenth and seventeenth-century cycle set in Ephesus, where the Saint is evidently posed to imitate Christ, a fairly unusual effect (at the beginning of the century Filippo Lippi in Florence had depicted him as an already old man in Ephesus).

In the New Testament (Gospels of Luke and Mark, Acts of the Apostles), John, fisherman and disciple of Jesus, is described as a strong, ambitious person. According to Christian tradition, the verses in the fourth Gospel that mention an unnamed 'loved disciple', who in particular witnessed the passion, death and resurrection of Christ, refer to him. Various New Testament verses are attributed to John which, if not written directly by him, are considered an expression of his theology: the fourth Gospel, three letters and the Revelation. The tradition that John lived a long time in Asia Minor, organising and leading the Christian community in Ephesus, dates from Ireneo of Lyons (second century), while Clement of Alexandria (pre 215) tells of his exile on the island of Patmos, inflicted on him by a Roman court. The apocryphal *Acts of John* tell of travels, miracles and the death of the saint, but the most important source for the literary and artistic portrayals remains the thirteenth-century *Golden Legend*. The iconography of the saint thus touches on various aspects of his long life, attributing numerous symbols to him (the book or scroll, the eagle, the chalice with the poisoned snake, the jar of oil) and portraying him in various guises (disciple, evangelist, apostle, bishop, martyr and exile).

In the places dedicated to the saint there is often a scene with a connection to the life of Christ: the most frequent is the *Crucifixion*, even more justified in the Scuola by its veneration for the relic. Indeed, he is found upright beneath the Cross on the Gothic reliquary and in the eighteenth-century stuccoes in the Sacristy. The addition of the *Transfiguration of Christ* to the Johannine cycle is less obvious: an evangelical episode in which John took part along with Peter and James. In this version by **Domenico Tintoretto**, a very young, fair-haired John is not looking toward the scene, but holds and looks at the reliquary, suggesting a less immediate connection between the two devotions than in the Crucifixions, but equally matched with the Johannine conception of the Passion as revelation of Glory.

Domenico Tintoretto
Transfiguration (detail), 1623

Stories of St John the Evangelist

The *Stories of St John the Evangelist*, taken from the apocryphal *Acts of John* and the *Golden Legend*, consist of three groups of works. The nucleus, commissioned after 1597, has come to us incomplete and is on the walls of the Chapter Room, along with unrelated works acquired separately after the closure. They are mainly very late works by Domenico Tintoretto, but are important because of the image of the saint presented as a champion of true religion against paganism.

Starting from the entrance in anti-clockwise direction:

1. Domenico Tintoretto, *St John destroys the temple of the goddess Diana in Ephesus with prayer* (1628). This fairly flat painting, a long way from the compositional and chromatic vibrancy typical of the earlier work of Jacopo's son, recounts a miracle taken from the Acts of John.

2. Sante Peranda, *Martyrdom of St John* (1605-6). According to the *Golden Legend*, the saint, deported from Ephesus to Rome during Domitian's persecution, was thrown into a cauldron of boiling oil, a martyrdom from which he escaped unharmed.

3. Andrea Vicentino, *Deposition* (end of sixteenth century). A fine example of Veneto mannerism following Tintoretto. It clearly does not belong to the Johannine cycle by subject or size (from a Belluno church, it is a state deposit of 1923).

4. Domenico Tintoretto, *Transfiguration* (1623). The only episode taken from the Gospel, with the significant variant of the saint (the young fair-haired man on the left) who does not actually take part in the scene with his companions Peter and James, but turns to look at the precious reliquary he is holding.

The Life of St John in Ephesus continues on the opposite wall:

5. Domenico Tintoretto, *St John converts the philosopher Crato* (from about 1626). The two figures argue about wealth, according to what is told in the *Golden Legend*.

6. Pietro Longhi (attributed to), *Adoration of the Magi* (1732-34). The faces have the pleasant features typical of this master of the small scene (not part of the series).

7. Domenico Tintoretto, *St John survives the cup of poison* (1623-26). The *Golden Legend* says that, after a revolt of the jewellers who sold amulets of Diana, the priest Aristodemo confronted the saint and proposed that he make a sacrifice to the goddess or drink a cup of poison from which two criminals had already drunk (the corpses in the centre). The saint drank, the poison went out in the form of a snake, and revived the two. Some clients are seen at bottom left.

8. Antonio Balestra (attributed to), *Adoration of the Shepherds* (eighteenth century). Unrelated to the cycle, in the Scuola since 1857.

9. Domenico Tintoretto, *St John Revives the Disciple Drusiana* (1626). Another episode from the *Acts of John*. The obscure funeral procession is not particularly effective, considering the illustrious Florentine precedents (Giotto and Filippo Lippi).

There are four further episodes on the back wall of the tribune, added in 1760 after the extension of the hall. The two tondi are by **Jacopo Guarana**, the two rectangular sections are by **Jacopo Marieschi** and recount some miracles performed by the saint in charming eighteenth-century scenes.

In the Oratory of the Cross there are two more episodes, attributed to the **school of Palma il Giovane** (end of sixteenth century): in addition to a *St John the Evangelist baptising a pagan priest*, the same episode as that recounted in the Chapter Room, the *Assumption of St John Evangelist* is interesting. It takes up one of the various traditions on the death of the saint, of whose destiny Christ had said to Peter 'what does it matter to you if I want him to stay until I return?', interpreted as meaning that John was not dead.

43

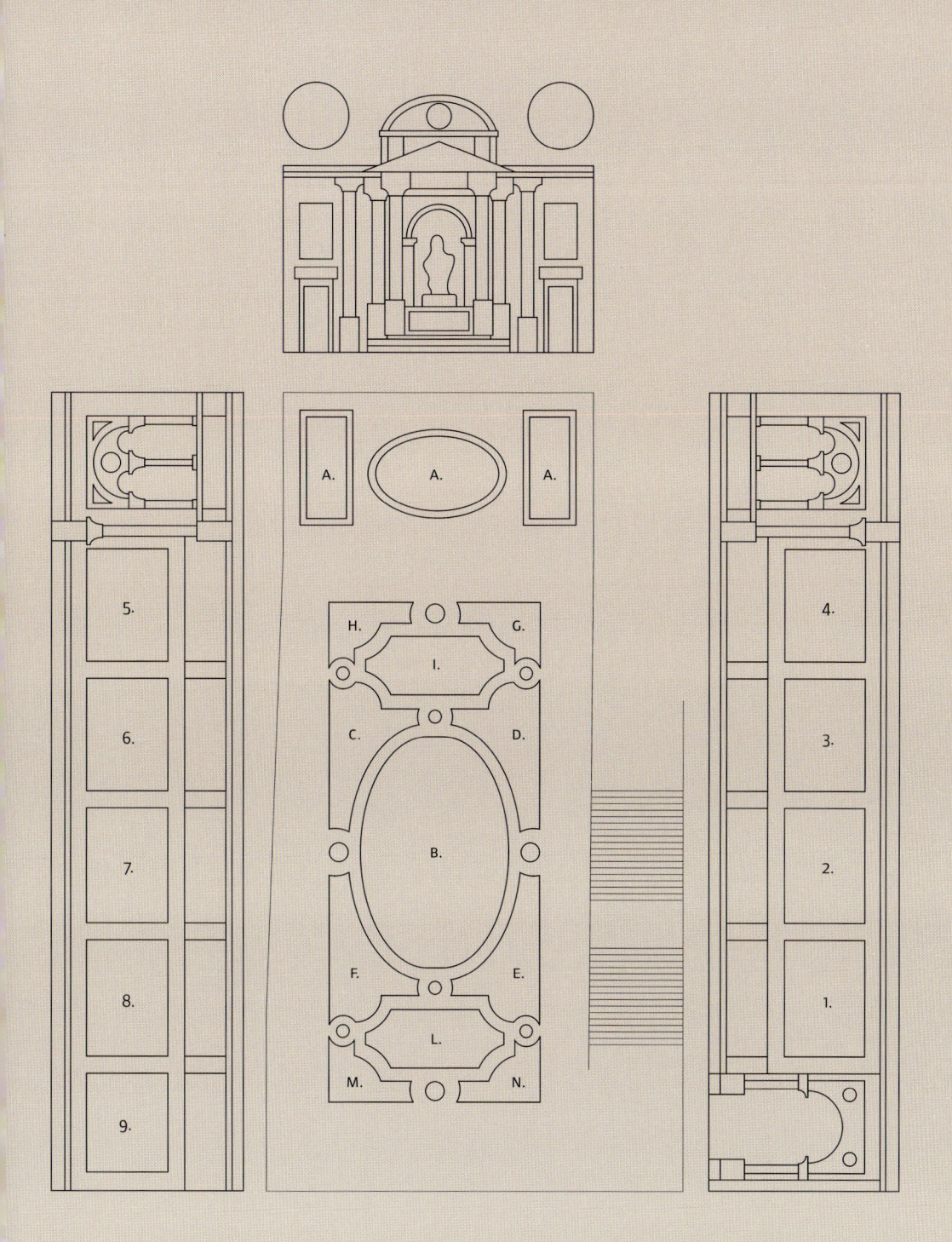

44

The Cycle of the *Apocalypse* (1760-62)

A. Edoardo Perini, *Three scenes of the Fight between Angels and Demons*. The first ceiling canvases were painted in 1732 for the tribune by Perini, who also painted the central oval, which was not appreciated and replaced.

B. Giuseppe Angeli, *Last Judgement* (previously known as the *Struggle with the Antichrist*). The central oval is not particularly effective. It was painted in 1761 by Angeli, former director of Piazzetta's workshop, during a downward phase of his production. In the centre, the not particularly expressive figure of Christ the Merciful Judge spreads his arms over the ranks of the damned (on the left) and the redeemed (on the right), with the usual flight of angels here slightly dispersed.

C-F. Gaspare Diziani, *St John Measures the Temple* (the angel hands John the rod for measuring the temple); *The Venerable Old Man with the Seven Lamps* (initial vision); *The Whore of Babylon*; *The Angel Chains the Dragon*. The four pendentives entrusted to Diziani (a painter engaged for the patrician residences of the Contarini, the Widman and the Rezzonico families) focus on some isolated figures, judiciously and scenically arranged and distinguished by bright colouring.

G-I. Jacopo Marieschi, *The Book of the Seven Seals*; *The Woman Crowned in Stars*; *St John Devours the Book*. The three sections towards the altar are by Marieschi, pupil of Gaspare Diziani and academic teacher at the peak of his career, who painted lively, bright compositions with jagged brush strokes. The complex mixtilinear central section takes up the introductory section of the Apocalypse, with St John taken up to heaven before the throne of the Lamb. The scene is interpreted as a kind of Glory of the Saint, quite in keeping with its place in front of the altar, reinforced by the three theological virtues on the cornice in the foreground.

L. Jacopo Guarana, *Vision of Seven Angels and Seven Vases*. In the mixtilinear section towards the oratory, Guarana, renowned for his grandiose compositional layouts, confidently plots various moments from the Revelation.

M-N. Giandomenico Tiepolo, *The Woman Dressed in the Sun*; *The Four Angels and the Four Evil Winds*. The corner sections towards the oratory are certainly the best in the cycle, in obviously Tiepolo colours and composition. His beautiful woman dressed in the sun, with the moon beneath her feet (from one of the most famous chapters of the Revelation) rises triumphant, having escaped the threats of evil thanks to the wings of the big eagle (symbol of the saint and figure in the story). The visionary nature of the scene is accentuated by the realism of the considerably foreshortened figure of John, crouching down and forced to look with his head back and nose up (such that his nostrils can be seen). The opposite section is a masterpiece of composition, the most uneven and difficult part of the ceiling, coinciding with an obtuse angle. In this narrow space, Tiepolo placed a good eight figures of angels and evil winds, arranging them into two groups (of six and two), at the edges also capturing a glimpse of clear sky at the centre, in which another pair of birds circles between the typical white and pink clouds. The blue depth is exalted by the figure of the central white angel, who rises with authority above the group of three brawny 'evil winds' pushed toward the corner by the incorporeal force of the two angels at the side. In a whirl of drapery, the white angel overpowers a dark 'evil wind', all muscles and blood, reddened by the vain attempt to emit the breath that swells up his cheeks. Reduced almost to a mask, the poor evil wind documents Giandomenico's dramatic liking for caricature and theatrical characterisation that so responded to the sensibilities of late eighteenth-century Venice.

Jacopo Guarana
Vision of Seven Angels and Seven Vases, 1762

Jacopo Marieschi
The Book of the Seven Seals, 1760

Giandomenico Tiepolo
The Four Angels and the Four Evil Winds, 1760

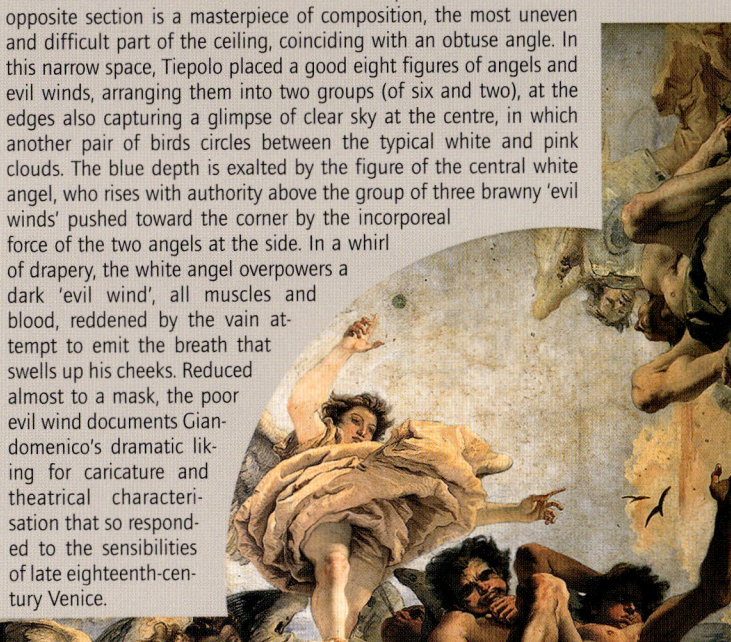

following pages:
Giuseppe Angeli
Last Judgement, 1761

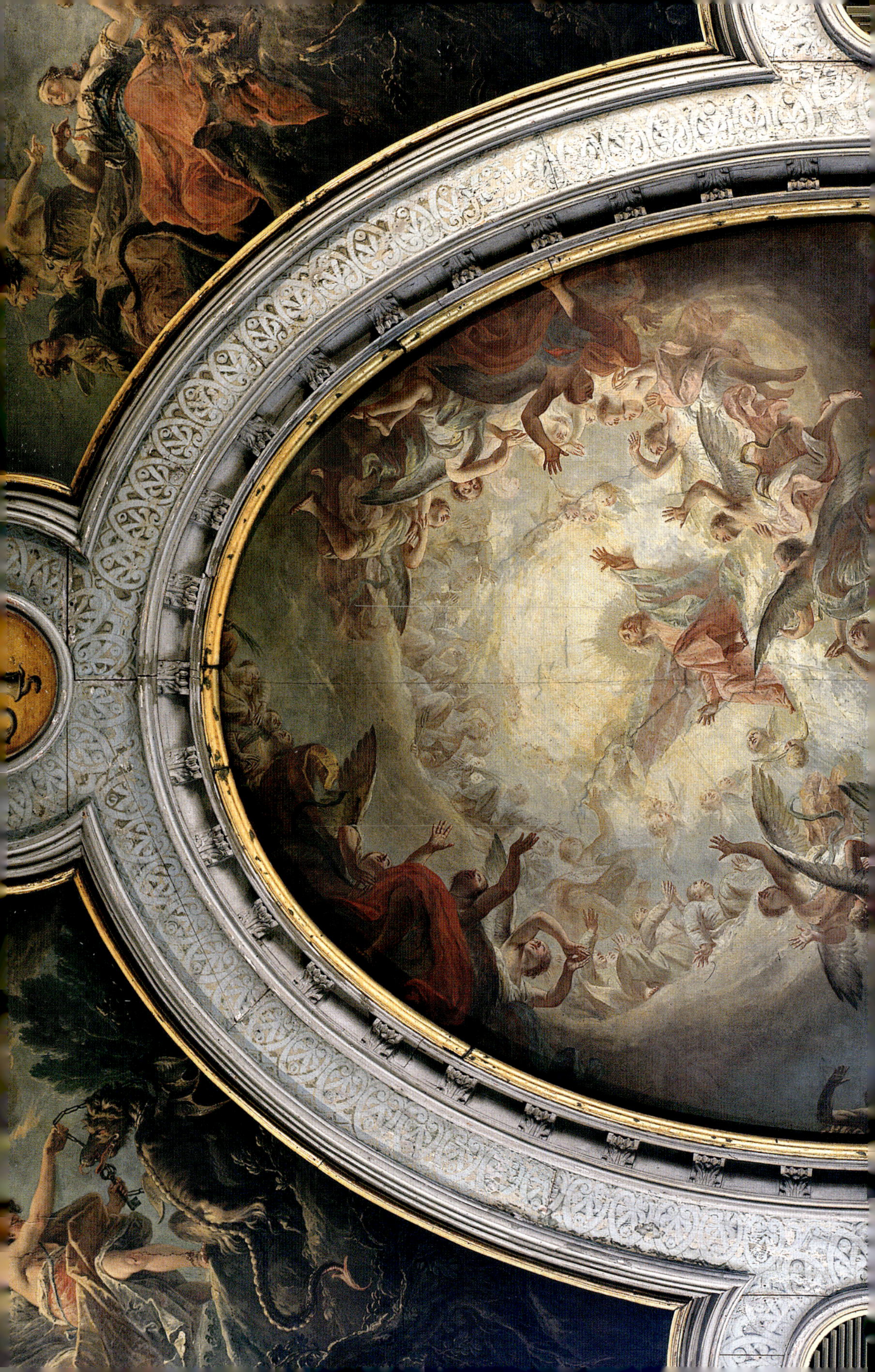

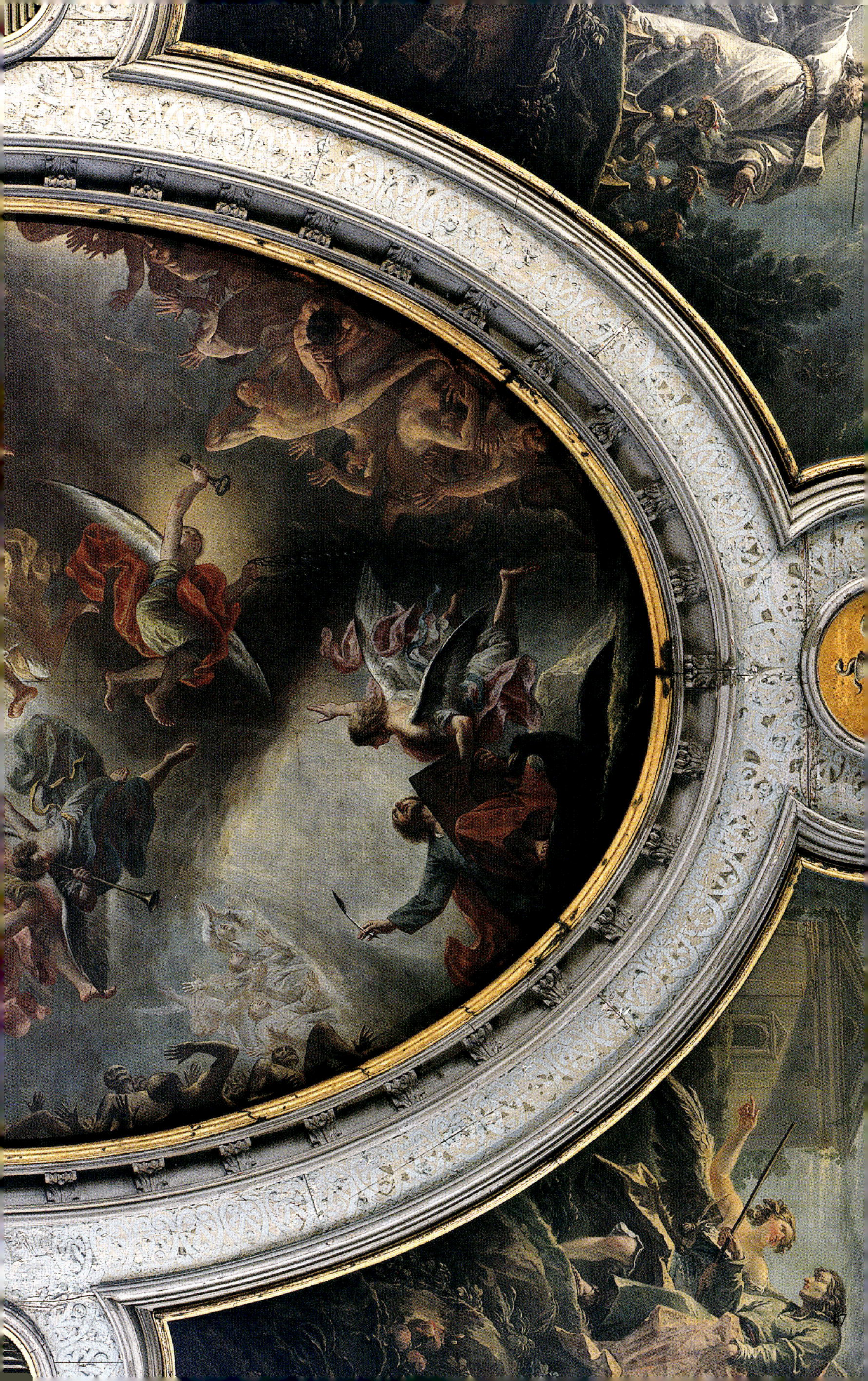

Stucco Rooms (Sacristy and Chancellery)

These two bright, discreet, matching rooms called the Stucco Rooms were built in 1757 to support the Chapter Room, each with three doors and three windows. Entirely decorated with elegant stuccoes by the Ticino masters **Antonio Adami** and **Francesco Re** with the assistance of the engraver **Matteo Bravi**, they retain the enchantment of eighteenth-century Venice. White figures and decorations on the walls and ceiling are interwoven on grounds of delicate pastel pink, blue-grey and pale green, typical of Venetian rococo. The decoration is centred on the high cavetto mouldings (between the cornice and ceiling) into which the four corners and the centre lines are inserted and on the overdoors; the ceilings are distinguished by a big central oval with picturesque allegories inspired by the same love of space and perspective tricks of the great Venetian painting tradition. The complex is completed by sober coloured fields and framed by strips with friezes slightly protuding from the walls. Lacking in baroque exuberance, the modelling is anyway very rich in ornamental themes and in framing of every kind, while the figurative bas reliefs are in elegant chiaroscuro. The traditional Venetian terrazzo floor, in brilliant shades of red and ochre, is enhanced with elegant ornamental motifs.

The two rooms are connected by a landing decorated in pink and yellow stuccoes with a *font* near the door to the Sacristy.

The Sacristy, on the left, offers a challenging iconographic programme developed in fine white stuccoes on yellow fields and dominated by a magnificent *Crucifixion* on the right wall. Surrounded by a majestic frame surmounted by a large shell, the three soaring figures of the Crucifix, Mary and John make up an intensely dramatic scene of undeniable pictorial effect. The iconography of the patron saint is significant: while Mary wraps herself in rough drapery with pained dignity, John reaches up with heroic pose, glorified by the dignity of being the chosen disciple to whom the dying Christ entrusted his mother, along with the testimony of the tradition of the apostles, symbolised by the book held in his left arm. The two *Seated female figures* in the side sections also celebrate the patron, holding the symbols of the saint: the eagle on the right and the palm and jar of oil on the left (alluding to the attempted martyrdom).

Two projecting *Eagles* are also positioned on the impost cornice, above the entrance door and on the opposite side, while on the green cavetto moulding four *Allegorical figures* alternate with *Putti* and, at the corners, four *Angels* are delicately posed with quill in hand. This is an unusual portrayal of the evangelists: Mark with the lion, John with the eagle, Luke with the easel (instead of the ox, alluding to Luke as the painter of the icon of the Virgin) and Mathew with the book (his attribute being an angel). On the ceiling, the green central oval presents a majestic allegory of *Faith*, symbolised by the robust woman with covered head and Greek profile, who leans her left arm on the Cross, while holding the radiant Eucharist (chalice and particle) in her right hand. Three clinging putti in a

**Antonio Adami
Francesco Re**
Crucifixion, 1757

**Antonio Adami
Francesco Re**
Allegory of Faith, 1757

crooked column lean out manneristically to take the weight, while two other adoring cherubs are respectively near the chalice and God (the triangle with the eye in the middle).

The Chancellery, on the right, is distinguished by an iconographic programme that refers to an ideal of administrative rectitude. In the middle of the ceiling there is an allegory of *Justice* intended as equity: seated on clouds pushed by putti, the graciously dressed female figure holds a scales on one side, and on the other a container from which coins fall in abundance, in a virtuoso cluster that ranges from high to very low, almost vanishing relief. At the four corners, the theological virtues of *Faith* (veiled woman with chalice and Cross), *Charity* (with children) and *Hope*, repeated twice (woman with the anchor and woman who turns her gaze upward) are held up by eagles in the round. There are more *Virtues* on the paired overdoors, while on the one above the entrance two *Putti* hold up the inscription with the date of the works, 1757. Above the impost cornice, *Four pairs of putti* holding the symbols of the Scuola (the crosier and chalice; the reliquary-Cross and a sword; the book and the quill; the scroll and the quill) lean on slightly protruding balconies decorated with elegant gilt rosette lattice.

In order to foster a more complete understanding of the historic and artistic aspects of the Scuola, a photographic reproduction in reduced scale of the famous cycle of paintings on the *Miracles of the Cross* has been placed in this room, formerly in the Oratorio della Croce and now in the Gallerie dell'Accademia.

The Relic of the Cross and the *Miracles*

The Scuola has since 1369 housed two fragments of wood believed to be relics of the Cross on which Jesus Christ died. In the Middle Ages and modern times Venice boasted numerous relics, that is, the mortal remains of people venerated as saints, or objects used by them, and also some relics of Christ's Passion, such as the blood and nails. Ownership of relics was considered prestigious, a source of spiritual richness and protection for the whole city, and strengthened its religious and political image. According to tradition, the Cross was found by St Helen, mother of the emperor Constantine (who issued the edict of tolerance that recognised the Christian religion in the Roman Empire) during a journey to Jerusalem between 327 and 329. Mother and son had two churches built, where the relics of wood were displayed to the faithful on 14 September 335. Stolen by the Persians of Cosroe II in 614, they were recovered by Heraclius, the Roman emperor of the East, in 628. As the Good Friday liturgy became established, recalling the passion and death of Christ, relics were distributed throughout the Christian world, such that the proliferation of fragments induced eighth-century theologians to claim that Christ's blood had made the wood imperishable and it could not be depleted no matter how many pieces of it were removed. The fragments that came to the Scuola were smuggled out of Jerusalem by some friars, who in 1360 gave them to the patriarch of Constantinople Pietro Tommaso. Entrusted to Filippo de Mezières in 1366, grand chancellor of the Order of Jerusalem and Cyprus, three years later they were sent by public deed to the guardian grande, Andrea Vendramin, and held in the Scuola until the Napoleonic closure in 1806. The last guardian grande, Giovanni Andrighetti, rescued the reliquary, which had been expropriated and sent for melting down at the mint, from state ownership. In 1871 his heirs offered it to the church of San Giovanni Evangelista, where it remained until 1929, when the Marcello family donated it to the patriarch of Venice, Cardinal Pietro La Fontaine, who returned it to the newly reconstituted Scuola Grande.

The Scuola has adopted 14 September as its patronal feast, the day of the worship of the Cross, during which the reliquary is taken in procession from the Scuola to the church. According to Catholic spirituality, the relic makes the place in which it is conserved and those who visit it participants in the holiness and grace of Christ, mindful that worshipping the Cross the Christian always and only adores the Crucifix, Christ the Saviour.

Vittore Carpaccio
Miracle of the Rialto Bridge
1494
Venice, Gallerie dell'Accademia

The Miracles of the Cross

The expectations of the important relic, received with great solemnity, were confirmed by a series of miraculous events between 1369 and 1480, immortalised in a famous cycle of teleri (i.e. paintings on big canvases mounted on frames, a wall technique suited to decoration in damp Venice), three of which are by **Gentile Bellini** and one by **Vittore Carpaccio**, the 'inventors of the Venetian urban view'. This colourful figurative account, played out on glimpses and views crowded with meticulously detailed people, expresses the religious and civic significance of the worship of this relic in Venetian life. The cycle, from which a *Miracle of the Vendramin Ships* by **Perugino** is missing (lost in the sixteenth century), was expropriated after the closure in 1806 and since 1820 has been in the Gallerie dell'Accademia.

Lazzaro Bastiani, *Offer of the Relic to the Scuola di San Giovanni Evangelista*. Painted after 1495, the canvas depicts the acceptance of the Cross donated by Filippo de Mezières at the Badoer complex, parts of which, later altered or destroyed, particularly the door opposite the church, are fairly freely interpreted.

Gentile Bellini, *Miracle at the San Lorenzo Bridge*. Signed and dated 1500, it shows a miracle confirming the brotherhood's ownership of the relic (according to a typical model of relic stories, similar to episodes in which the saint makes his own body be found in a specific place): the reliquary, featured in the procession for the Feast of St Lawrence (the monastery is on the other side of the city), falls into the water due to the crush, but evades all rescuers, priest included, apart from the guardian grande, the same Andrea Vendramin who had received it in 1369. The importance of the episode is sanctioned by the presence among the worshippers of Caterina Cornaro, the noble Venetian queen of Cyprus, with her ladies, kneeling on the left, while the five people on the right would be members of the Scuola. It is no mere chance that the *penelo* (the identifying banner of the Scuola) stands out in the middle, while the reliquary held above the water is evidently the one still housed in the Oratorio della Croce.

Giovanni Mansueti, *Miracle of the Daughter of Benvegnudo da San Polo*. Paralysed from birth, the daughter of Benvegnudo was healed at the touch of three candles previously placed near the relic. In the 1502 canvas the episode is set in sumptuous and crowded proto-Renaissance architecture, cleverly composed on several levels both in height and depth.

Gentile Bellini, *Miracle of the Merchant Jacopo de' Salis during the Procession of St Mark*. The most famous of the paintings, signed and dated 1496, was intended to show the miraculous healing of the seriously wounded son of a Brescian merchant, Jacopo de' Salis, but turned into an authentic snapshot of St Mark's square as it was prior to the sixteenth-century alterations (paving in red brick and prior to the building of the clock tower and the Procuratie Nuove) and of the basilica with all its original mosaics (of which only those on the first arch on the right still remain). In the foreground, the brothers take part in the ducal procession in honour of St Mark (25 April) with an elegant gilt *solèr* on which the canopy covered reliquary is inserted.

Giovanni Mansueti, *Miracle in Campo San Lio*. Along with another urban scene (with the strange sign 'casa da fitar ducati 5' on the right), this canvas of 1494 shows a practice typical of the scuole: accompanying deceased brothers to their burial. In this case the pole refuses to go over the bridge to go and get the body in the presence of the relic, for which the deceased had shown little devotion, so the priest has to lend one of his Crosses. The preparatory drawing is by Gentile Bellini, of whom Mansueti declares himself a follower in the scroll held by the man with his hand on his beret on the left.

Benedetto Rusconi, called Diana, *Miracle of the Son of Ser Alvise Finetti*. The boy fallen from the upper floor and miraculously healed is shown languishing in his mother's arms. The small group of witnesses and the mock-classical architectural ruins are atypical of the urban views painted by Bellini and Carpaccio. They are inspired rather by the new models of Giorgione and Lotto (first decade of the sixteenth century).

Gentile Bellini, *Miracle of Pietro de' Ludovici*. Painted in 1501, the canvas refers to the healing of a sufferer of quartan fever, thanks to the touch of a candle previously held near the relic. The worshipper kneels before a fanciful temple of St John (represented by the altar piece and symbolised by the eagle in the central lunette) derived from drawings by Jacopo, Gentile's father. The design of the Scuola doorway onto the courtyard, built by 1512, has also been attributed to Gentile Bellini by analogy with these forms.

Vittore Carpaccio, *Miracle of the Rialto Bridge*. Francesco Querini, patriarch of Grado, heals a person possessed by showing him the relic. The story is divided into three sections: procession over the bridge (still a wooden drawbridge until 1524), entrance of the patriarch, and the healing on the loggia: three sequences framed within a grand portrait of Venice showing the extraordinary descriptive skill of the 'painter of stories'. Painted by 1494, this canvas of almost four by four metres is an extraordinary tribute to the city (with gondolas, roof terraces, hotels, warehouses, hanging signs and laundry, bell towers, chimneys and above all its citizens) and took the very heart of the city, Rialto, before the relic held in the small, secluded oratory.

Gentile Bellini
Miracle at the San Lorenzo Bridge, 1500
Venice, Gallerie dell'Accademia

Oratory of the Cross

This room, which has housed the famous Relic of the Cross since the end of the fourteenth century, was also altered during the eighteenth-century restorations. These changed its spatial layout, by removing a door and opening a biforate window towards the hall, and its decorations, definitively changing their meaning. The small room had previously been decorated with the famous pictorial cycle on the *Miracles of the Cross* (1494-1502) by **Gentile Bellini**, **Vittore Carpaccio** and others, now in the Gallerie dell'Accademia (smaller scale reproduction in the Chancellery). These very big masterpieces completely lined the walls and celebrated the Relic of the Cross held by the Scuola (solemn presentation, procession in St Mark's square, healing and other miraculous episodes) with flamboyant richness. The realism of the figures and the urban settings for which they are so renowned virtually brought the city into the room and crowded it with people taken from daily life and from civic rituals. Entering through the small doors it was possible to emerge in this real Venice, pulsating in all its material and spiritual richness, in a sign of reciprocal glorification and affiliation between city and relic.

Between 1784 and 1788 **Bernardino Maccaruzzi**, a student of Massari, continued his teacher's work of transforming the medieval oratory, previously the heart of associative and public worship, into an intimate and elegant chapel, with soft, refined tones, possibly more in keeping with a private patrician chapel and certainly the expression of a less civic and more abstract piety.

The superb *stuccoed ceiling* is distinguished by its delicate greens, blues and pastel pinks, softly brightened by the gilding in a perfect example of the unique style of Venetian stucco between rococo and neo-classicism. A greater solemnity is bestowed on these, compared to the Stucco Rooms, by the extensive use of gold, highlighting grounds in the corners and above the windows, repeated framing lines, elegant vegetal bouquets and sealed with elaborate frames. The symbols of St John (eagle, crosier and chalice of poison) and the Cross are shown in small blue tondi; at the corners some *putti* on small balusters hold up elegant monochrome medallions (ochre on sepia) depicting cherubs with the symbols of Christ's passion: the crown of thorns, the spear with sponge, nails, ropes and chalice. They are by **Francesco Maggiotto** (1738-1805), who also painted the central canvas with the *Triumph of the Cross*, carried by some angels in a slightly rigid and fairly cold devotional composition. Between the entrance and the biforate window, an elegant *composition of white stucco* on blue marbling reproduces the form of the old reliquary, surrounded by a radiant aura and held up by three

Francesco Maggiotto
Triumph of the Cross
1784-1788

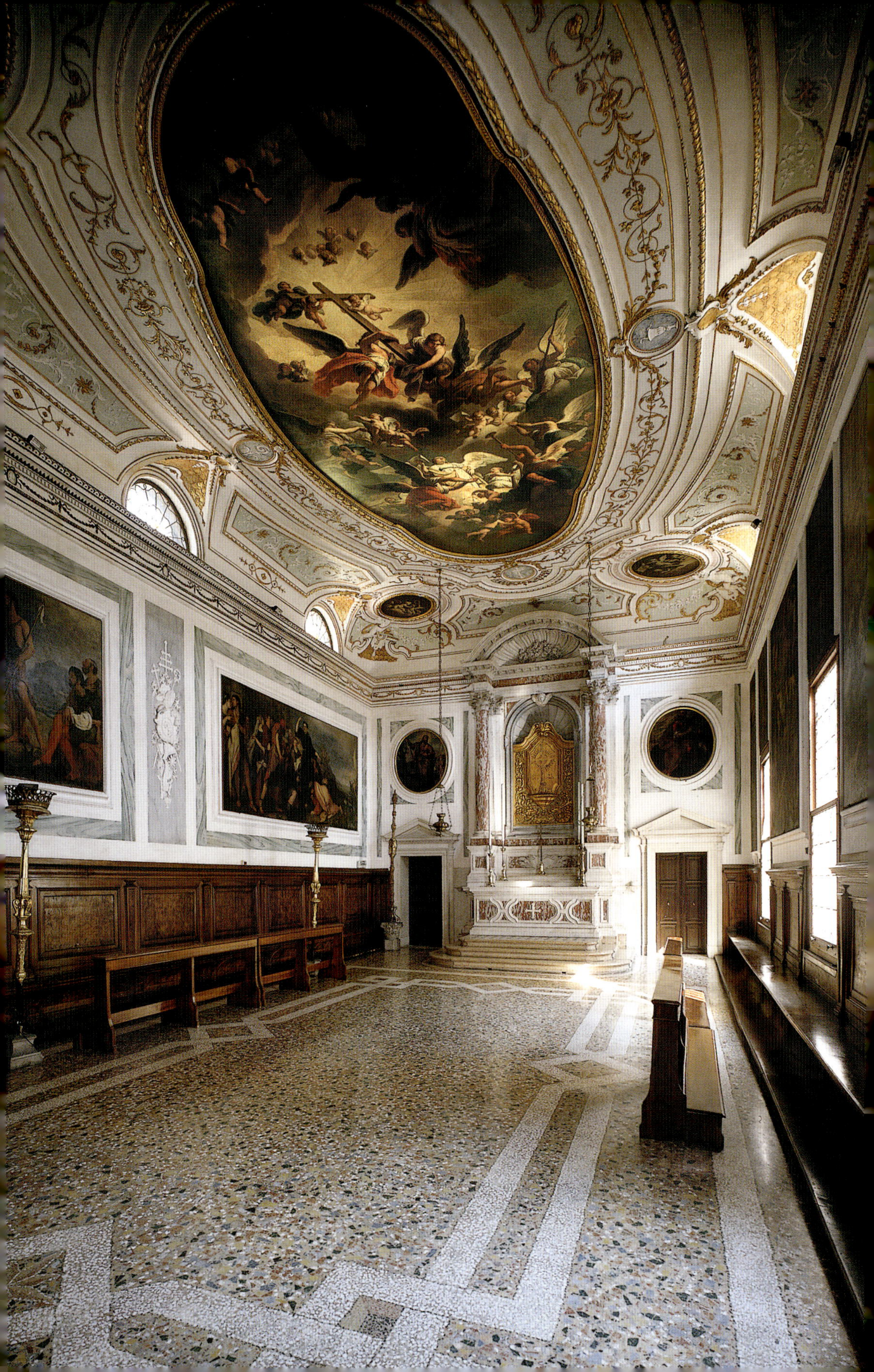

angels, above the Johannine symbols (the crosier, eagle and book).
On the floor, the prized Venetian terrazzo repeats the colouring of the ceiling in brighter tones. The *altar*, in imposing, variegated red marble, was completed by an altarpiece depicting *St John Worshipping the Cross*, now in a room on the ground floor. It was replaced by a gilt shrine with the dates 1806-1929, made to mark the recovery of the relic after the vicissitudes following closure of the Scuola.

The walls are lined with works that are not part of the eighteenth-century decoration and were put here to replace the cycle on the *Miracles*. On the wall with the windows, four canvases from the **Veneto school of the late sixteenth century** (possibly the workshop of Palma il Giovane): the *Annunciation* and the *Announcing Angel* at the sides, while in the middle are two that continue the cycle dedicated to the life of the patron of the Scuola, formerly on the walls of the Chapter Room, with the episodes *St John the Evangelist Baptises a Pagan Priest* and the *Assumption of St John the Evangelist*. The remaining pictures are mainly works on deposit of various periods and origins: at the sides of the altar, *St Luke* and *St James the Great* by **Gaspare Rem** (1542-1617); above the windows, *St Mathew* and *St Andrew* (**Veneto school, late sixteenth century**) and *The Samaritan at the Well* (eighteenth century); above the door, *Hagar and Ishmael*, attributed to the painter **Elisabetta Lazzarini** (eighteenth century); above the biforate window, panels with *Scenes from the life of a saint*; on the wall two canvases attributed to **Giovanni Segala** (1663-1717), separated by a nineteenth-century stucco decoration with ecclesiastical symbols.

Stuccoes in the Oratory
1784-88

The reliquary and the processional pole

The superb *Reliquary-Cross* in rock crystal and gilded silver, a masterpiece of Venetian Gothic goldsmithing (1371), is kept in the altar in the Oratory. Its cross shape follows the high medieval tradition of the first reliquaries made for fragments of the Cross, but the whole piece depicts a complete crucifixion scene, the climax and synthesis of the redemption. The pentagonal crystal case at the top contains the two slivers of dark wood, placed in the form of a cross, believed to be fragments of the Cross on which Christ died. Immediately below, a large red stone recalls the blood of the sacrifice; at the sides there are two kneeling angels, while an angel at the top holds Veronica's veil. Four other precious blue stones on a rich decoration of leaves and vines are set around the central Crucifix. Half figures of angels and prophets with haloes and scrolls surround the arms of the Cross, while the figures of Mary and St John stretch out on two projecting branches at the sides. The figure of a Franciscan saint (worship of the Cross is typical of Franciscan spirituality) appears in the central niche, while the niches of the big hexagonal knot, normally used to contain figures of saints, are closed by coloured glazing, because the iconographic programme continued in the decoration of the processional pole. As this is an astylar Cross, the non-exposed side is also decorated, with a St John who protects two kneeling brothers with his open cloak.

The Reliquary-Cross was carried in procession on the extraordinary late fourteenth-century *wooden pole*, possibly the oldest object of its kind remaining in Venice. Almost three metres tall, it is gilded with gold leaf on a blue field and consists of a supporting element in pine with seven inlaid knots of arolla pine and a big hexagonal niche that takes up the gothic forms of the reliquary: six niches on spiral columns, with a crown in the form of shells, cusps and foliage. The figures of saints that were certainly housed there and completed the reliquary, according to the traditional iconography of astylar Crosses (for example the later Cross of the Scuola Grande di San Teodoro, now in the Gallerie dell'Accademia), here followed unusually in the two pieces, have been lost.

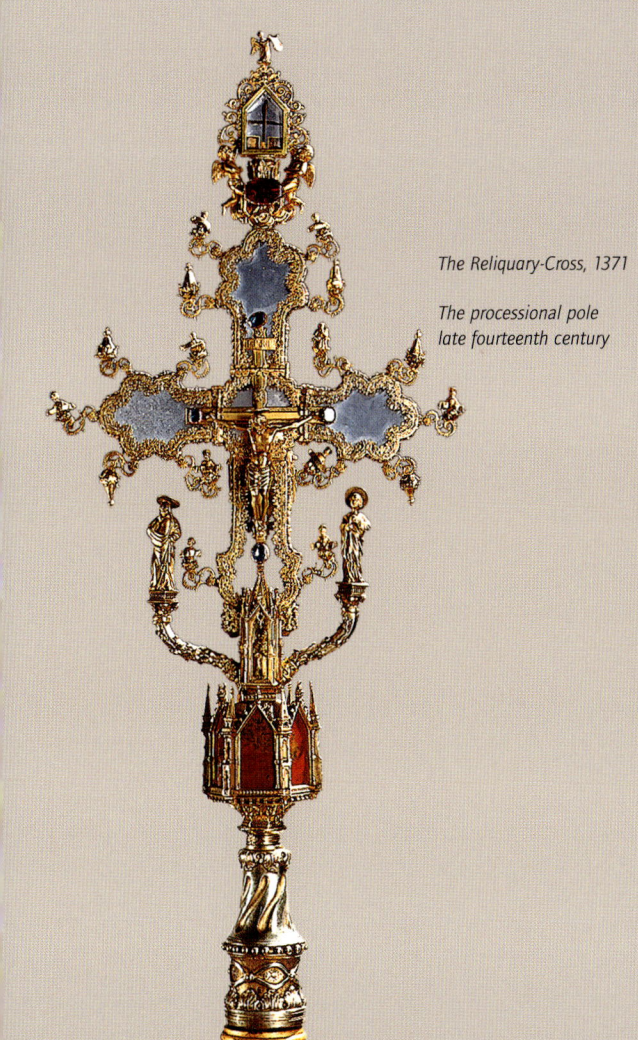

The Reliquary-Cross, 1371

The processional pole late fourteenth century

The Albergo

first floor

There is direct access from the Oratory of the Cross to the Albergo (or from outside, by a staircase from the courtyard). This was the name given in all the *scuole* to the room used for assemblies of the *Banca* and *Zonta*, the association's governing bodies (*albergo* is meant as headquarters, not as accommodation for the poor or pilgrims, which was on the ground floor). It is a small, square room where the eighteenth-century pattern is interrupted by a return to the mid-sixteenth century. The members sat in the thirteen places built into the *wooden panelling*, decorated with austere geometric inlays, simple but distinctive for each seat. They are surrounded by a magnificent decoration made after 1540, left intact by the eighteenth-century restorers but unfortunately seriously mutilated after the Napoleonic closure. The ceiling, now bare with simple exposed beams, was decorated with a composition of paintings in a gilt frame, at the centre of which was a painting by Titian with *St John in Patmos*, the start of a rich iconographic programme on the Apocalypse.

The four impressive canvases by **Jacopo Palma il Giovane** remain on the bare walls, of which the most striking is the one on the wall opposite the oratory, representing the vision of *The Four Horsemen of the Apocalypse* (1581-82). A 'real' foreground can be clearly distinguished, where the elderly saint with pen and inkhorn sits between rocks and vegetation. He is almost gripping or protecting the book, in which he is writing what appears to him behind in a whirl of clouds and bodies: Plague (with a bow on a white horse), War (with armour on a red horse), Famine (with scales on a black horse) and Death (on a green horse) carry away various people, followed by Hell, represented as a sea monster with open jaws that swallow up the victims. This figure taken from the famous etching by Albrecht Dürer has its pendant on the diagonal in the eagle of St John with outstretched wings. Heir to the extraordinary Venetian painting of the sixteenth century (Veronese, Titian, Tintoretto), Palma il Giovane was still an uncertain part of the highly demanded 'Veneto school' in the early 1580s, as may be noted in the other paintings, though not recently restored. The *Woman Crowned in Stars* between the windows suffers from a certain lack of depth (the sword of the angel who has come down to defend her rests carelessly on the dragon's tail) and is rather confused, even though the *Exterminating Angels* on the opposite wall are vaguely Michelangelesque. The *Signed by the Cross* (post 1582) on the wall towards the oratory is significant. The painter has managed to show us his clients between angels variously occupied in the sky and crowded ranks of those redeemed by the sign of the Cross: the members of the associative oligarchy who sat in the benches beneath. Obviously absent among the victims of the exterminations in the other episodes, the faces of those who guided the brotherhood in the golden period of the Scuole appear in the first row of those saved by the Cross. This ambitious hope had its basis in the works of charity to the needy (the naked and therefore allegorical figure of a poor person in the foreground, is covered with a striped fabric symbolising marginalisation, but is incongruously brawny in tribute to the dictates of mannerism) and its pledge in the wood of the Cross housed right behind this wall.

Jacopo Palma il Giovane
The Signed by the Cross
post 1582

Jacopo Palma il Giovane
The Four Horsemen
of the Apocalypse, 1581-82

Franciscus Pinsis
Madonna Platytera and Saints
fourteenth century

This room also has a big panel from the early fourteenth century, with a very ornate original frame found in the sacristy of the adjacent church, overturned as a board for the flooring. It is a rare example of the beginnings of Venetian painting, signed 'Franciscus pinsis' (sic), an artist not identified with any of the few known masters of that period. In the middle is a *Madonna Platytera*, a symbolic form popular in the thirteenth century in areas of Byzantine influence, from which the naturalist Renaissance model of the Virgin of Birth was to develop. The Christ child triumphant in vesica is in the centre of the oval half figure of the praying, welcoming Virgin (alluding to her identification with the Church). The double frontal pose with open arms has considerable impact, expressing an organic link between son and mother, whose face has a sweet charm. At the sides, the complete but reduced figures of saints give the composition an archaising tone, though these are also marked by portrait elements and drapery referring to Gothic styles. On the left, St Peter and St John the Baptist; on the right St John the Evangelist. The panel has evidently been cut and was probably completed by a St Paul; a similar group of saints is also found in the *Madonna of Humility* (i.e. nursing) painted by **Giovanni da Bologna** for the Scuola in the 1380s. Expropriated and now in the Accademia, it also shows a group of kneeling brothers below the Virgin, with cowl, scourges and banner; a composition that recalls the 1349 relief in the courtyard. The three works overall document the brothers' Marian devotion, stated several times in the *Mariegola*: 'che tutte quele cose le qual da mo' avanti per la nostra Scuola ordenaremo, sia a l'honor de Dio e della soa dolce mare Madona sancta Maria' (chapter III).

Titian in the Scuola di San Giovanni Evangelista

Titian made a significant contribution to the Scuola. He was engaged to decorate the ceiling of the new Albergo, and in 1544 visited the almost completed room and expressed his opinion on the arrangement of the canvases in the adjacent Oratory, which were cut to fit around the new doors. The ceiling was painted between 1546 and 1548 and consists of 21 paintings in a gilt lime frame. They were dismantled after the Napoleonic closure, then went to the Accademia in 1812 but without their frame, entirely destroyed, and one painting, lost. The very poorly conserved central canvas was sold to a Turin art merchant in 1818. Long considered lost and known only from an eighteenth-century engraving (shown on an easel), the work was bought by the Kress foundation in 1954 and then went to the National Gallery of Art in Washington. The remaining panels are still on deposit at the Accademia, some exhibited in the Quadreria. The group was recomposed in 1990 for the big exhibition on Titian, in which a possible reconstruction was attempted.

The central canvas, a stout *St John in Patmos*, captures the saint turning 'to see the voice' at the beginning of the apocalyptic visions. The twisting of the figure seen from below, with asymmetrical knees and outstretched arms, proclaims the taste for spatial illusionism, movement and mass that was then in vogue in Venice. The surrounding panels, to which the workshop also contributed, represented the symbols of the evangelist (a tradition that reworks a vision of the Apocalypse), as well as heads of cherubs, masks of satyrs and female faces. Titian painted another celebrated commemorative work for the Vendramin family (who held it until 1636 when they sold it to Anton Van Dyck), now in the National Gallery, London. It depicts the descendants of Andrea Vendramin, the guardian grande of 1369 (Gabriele Vendramin, art collector, his brother Andrea Vendramin and his seven children) in the act of paying homage to the Relic of the Cross in its easily recognisable Gothic reliquary. The dismay at the loss of these works goes beyond their importance to the Scuola: given the limited number of works by Titian remaining in Venice, it would have been a privilege to have been able to admire them just a few steps from his *Assumption* in the Frari.

Titian
St John in Patmos
1546-48
Washington, National Gallery of Art

Archive, or Guarana Room

An additional room for the administrative work of the Scuola was added at the end of the eighteenth-century alterations (entered from the Albergo, across the landing). Originally designed as the Archive and Council Room, it is now named after **Jacopo Guarana**, to whom the frescoes on the ceiling and above the doors are attributed. In an airy combination with the stuccoes, these frescoes on planks of wood (a technique typical of the late eighteenth century) offer an additional variant of the decorative style of the time: after the 'complete' stuccoes in the Chancellery and the Sacristy, and the solution in the Oratory with canvases and stuccoes, this room, too, is distinguished by the elegance and lightness of oval lines and pale colours. In the large frescoed tondo in the middle of the ceiling, *St John the Evangelist* is in the act of writing the Gospel, surrounded by three putti and an angel, along with the inevitable eagle. The white stuccoes on gilt ovals feature the symbols of the Scuola: from the entrance, in anti-clockwise direction, the *Chalice* with serpent, the *Crosier*, the *Eagle* with the books and the *Reliquary Cross*. At the corners, another four white ovals contain female figures, allegories of the virtues necessary for those who administered the Scuola: *Prudence*, with serpent and mirror; *Justice*, with sword and scales; *Temperance*, with a *putto* holding a vase from which water flows; and *Strength*, with a branch and a crown of oak leaves, accompanied by a lion. On the three frescoed overdoors, *Consilium*, *Concordia* and *Diligentia*, identified by the respective scrolls, complete the ideal of good government that had guided the ancient brotherhood for more than five centuries.

Jacopo Guarana
Diligentia, 1762

Jacopo Guarana
Consilium, 1762

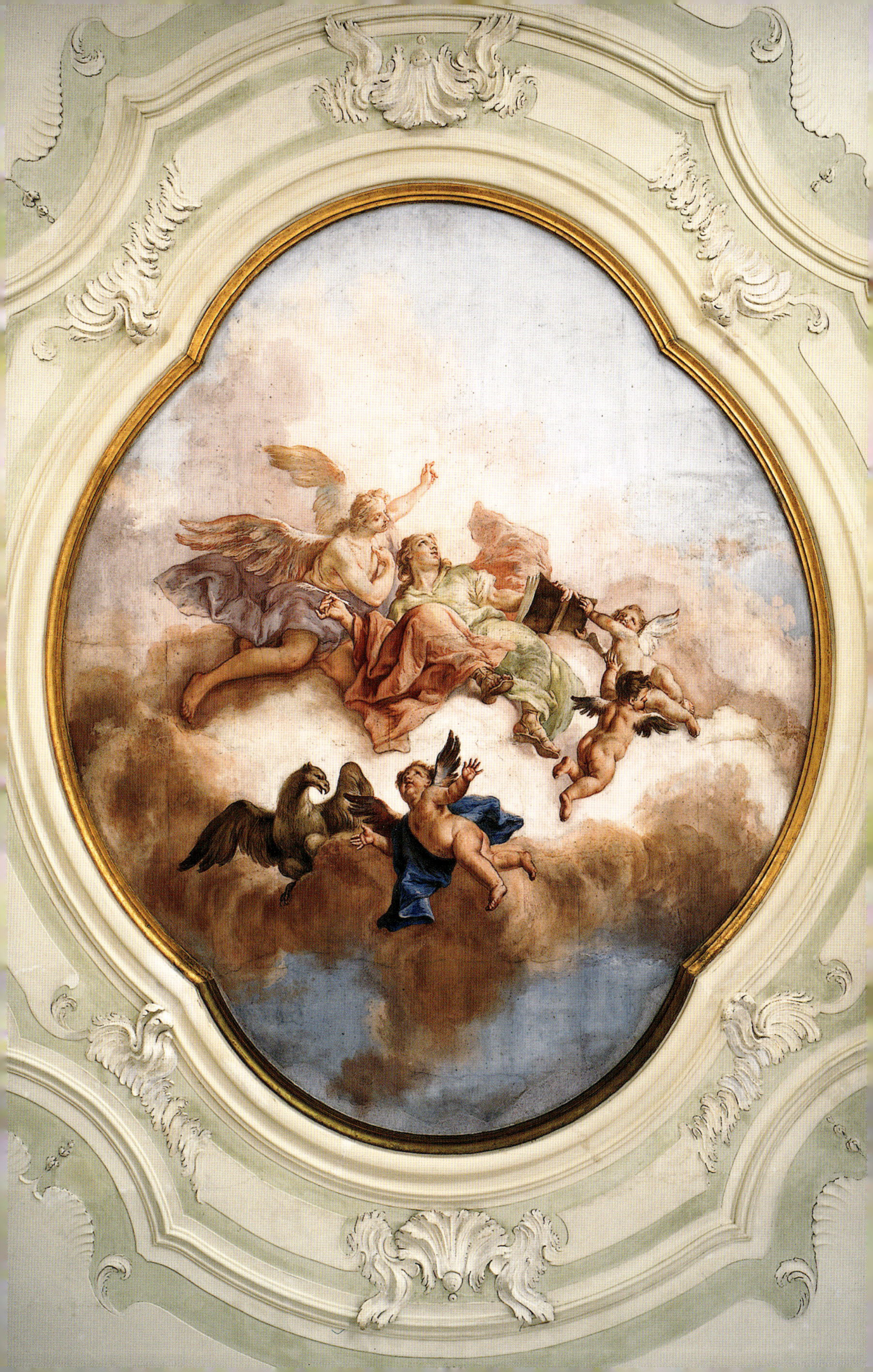

Essential bibliography

Sommario di Memorie, ossia descrizione succinta delli quadri esistenti nella veneranda Scola Grande di San Giovanni Evangelista, in Venetia 1787.

LORENZETTI G., *La Scuola Grande di San Giovanni Evangelista a Venezia*, Venice, Fantoni, 1929.

MASSARI A., *Giorgio Massari architetto veneziano del Settecento*, Vicenza, Neri Pozza Editore, 1971.

PIGNATTI T. (edited by), *Le scuole di Venezia*, Milan, Electa, 1981.

PULLAN B., *La politica sociale della Repubblica di Venezia 1500-1620*, vol. I, Rome, Il Veltro, 1982.

SEMI F., *Gli ospizi di Venezia*, Venice, Helvetia, 1983.

PAZZI P., *La chiesa di San Giovanni Evangelista a Venezia*, Venice, Tipolitografia Armena, 1985.

Venezia restaurata 1966-1986: la campagna dell'UNESCO e l'opera delle organizzazioni private, Milan, Electa, 1986.

Tiziano, exhibition catalogue, Venice, Marsilio, 1990.

Piero della Francesca. La Madonna del Parto. Restauro e iconografia, exhibition catalogue, Venice, Marsilio, 1993.

FILLITZ H., MORELLO G. (edited by), *Omaggio a San Marco. Tesori dell'Europa*, exhibition catalogue, Milan, Electa, 1994.

Restituzioni 95. Catalogo. Banco Ambrosiano Veneto, 1995.

NEPI SCIRÈ G. (edited by), *Gallerie dell'Accademia di Venezia*, Milan, Electa, 1998.

DE VITO F., *Venezia. Itinerari spirituali. Guida alla scoperta dei luoghi sacri*, Milan, Edizioni San Paolo, 2002.

SIMEONE G.A. (edited by), *La Mariegola della Scuola Grande di San Giovanni Evangelista a Venezia (1261-1457)*, Venezia, Scuola Grande di San Giovanni Evangelista, 2003.

BELLAVITIS G. (a cura di), *La Scuola grande di San Giovanni Evangelista e l'arte del restauro di Venezia*, Venice, Ateneo Veneto, 2003.

FOGLIATA M., SARTOR M.L., *L'arte dello stucco. Storia, tecnica, metodologie della tradizione veneziana*, Treviso, Antilia, 2004.

Giovanni Maria Morlaiter
St John the Evangelist
1732-33

Photolithography
Fotolito Veneta, San Martino Buonalbergo (Verona)

Printed by
Grafiche Nardin, Ca' Savio - Cavallino - Treporti (Venezia)
for Marsilio Editori® s.p.a. in Venezia

EDITION	YEAR
10 9 8 7 6 5 4 3 2	2010 2011 2012 2013 2014